KU-022-440

ACKNOWLEDGMENTS

This book is dedicated to all the New Users who became Power Users on their own while I mostly just watched. They inspired me by reflecting upon the need for entry-level DOS tutorials, all the time bootstrapping their own skill and knowledge. They taught themselves DOS, proving that it can be done. These are just some of them:

Michael Herman
Ron Skipper
Judy Stevens (who became a hacker, too)
Pat Wickersham

teach yourself... DOS

AL STEVENS

ADVANCED COMPUTER BOOKS

MIS: PRESS

A Subsidiary of
Henry Holt and Co., Inc.

First edition—1989

ISBN 1-55828-021-9

Library of Congress Catalog Card Number: 89-12124

Printed in the United States of America

20   19   18   17   16   15   14   13   12

MIS:Press books are available at special discounts for bulk
purchases for sales promotions, premiums, fund-raising, or
educational use. Special editions or book excerpts can
also be created to specification.
For details contact:
Special Sales Director, MIS:Press,
a subsidiary of Henry Holt and Company, Inc.,
115 West 18th Street, New York, New York 10011.

To the memory of Kent Porter.

TABLE OF CONTENTS

FOREWORD

In the spring of last year, my pal Ron Skipper called me. Ron is a 747 captain for an international charter operation. His has been a life of waste and hedonism, traveling to exotic places, living in the farthest reaches, partaking of all that man and nature have to offer, and generally having his way with the pleasures of the good earth. The examples set by Ron Skipper are removed from everything that we are taught is civilized and proper, and for that reason he has been suspect and envied far and abroad for most of his adult life. So much for the life and times of Ron Skipper.

Ron's call was bad news. The good life was at its end. The Federal Aviation Administration's Designated Medical Examiner heard Ron's heart knocking when it should have been tocking, and his flying days for the big paychecks were over. Ron, newly idle and with no marketable skills other than the clipped wings of a big bird jockey, was about to undertake his memoirs. To that end, he purchased a PC/AT clone and WordPerfect and enrolled in an adult education creative writing class.

But Ron did not call me to bemoan the loss of his former excesses and style or to boast of his new career as a soon-to-be celebrated author. He called because I use and write about PCs, and he had some problems. Ron couldn't get his PC to work. I agreed to fix it in exchange for one of his globally notorious dinners.

As it turned out, Ron's PC was working fine. He couldn't get it to work because he did not understand DOS, the Disk Operating System. He had spent his first day hammering out accounts of his tender years and had dutifully saved the results into the PC the way the computer salesperson had showed him. Then, weary from the day's hack, he turned off the PC and retired with visions of literary receptions and guest appearances on "Donahue," little dreaming that on the morrow his work would be lost, vanished into the vapor. The next morning, staring at an empty screen and sitting with fingers poised and trembling, Ron could but wonder about the whereabouts and fate of what he had written.

To a writer, this is panic. The loss of a day's work is the greatest of losses; the creative juices will never flow in those precise same directions through those exact same channels. With a bit of searching and a lot of reassuring, I found the lost chapter and showed Ron where it was and attempted to explain how it got there. He is a quick study and wants to learn. The dinner was excellent, too.

The next day, we scoured the bookstores for a good tutorial on DOS. We found several books, and Ron bought one. He reported back that while the book usually got him the answer he sought, the level of detail was far too advanced for what he really needed. Over drinks at Dino's, we concluded together that what the DOS tenderfoot really needs is a layered approach to a tutorial—just enough to get going, and then, as experience allows, a spoon-feeding of more advanced knowledge. The result of our mutual conclusion is this little book.

The saga has a medium-to-good ending. Ron Skipper has no Pulitzer Prize yet, but he can get the PC up and running successfully and loses his work no more often than once a month now. And as for the good part, I have written this book, and you have purchased it. With it you will teach yourself DOS. You will teach yourself at a graduated pace — the way any complex subject should be taught. You will teach yourself enough the first time out to allow yourself to use the PC in the simplest ways. You will be able to move around through the DOS file system, and you will be able to execute DOS commands and your other programs. Then, as your experience with DOS grows, you will learn more advanced DOS concepts and commands.

WHAT TEACH YOURSELF DOS DOES NOT TEACH

Teach Yourself DOS is not a DOS reference manual in the truest sense. You got one of those when you purchased DOS. A reference manual assumes that you already know what a Disk Operating System is and what the commands are. When you want to know the details of a command, you will look up the command in an alphabetic list and read about the command's syntax and effects. That's fine for the veteran user who knows the commands and knows what commands are. But the rookie needs more help than that. A rookie not only does not know the commands, he or she might not know that a PC has commands and what they could be. If you do not know what a disk directory is, how can you know that you can display one — or that you want to?

Teach Yourself DOS is not a comprehensive treatment of DOS. It does not teach you everything there is to know about DOS. As a novice user of DOS, you do not need to know it all.

Teach Yourself DOS is not a hardware primer. It does not tell you where the sectors are on a floppy disk or what the keyboard looks like. You do not need to know about such things as File Allocation Tables, Boot Blocks, or Interleave Factors. Who cares how many heads the disk drive has? When and if you become a Power User, you can care about those things. For now, their explanations would either bore or confuse you, and you do not need them. You do not need me telling you what your hardware looks like either. If you have a PC and want to know what the keyboard and mouse (if you have one) look like, cast your eyes downward. There they are.

This book is not a programmer's manual. Every operating system has features for programmers alone. DOS, for example, has programs called BASICA, LINK, DEBUG, and EXE2BIN. If you are a programmer, you will find these programs to be of use. This book, however, is not for programmers exclusively, and it has no place for subjects that only a programmer would understand.

WHAT TEACH YOURSELF DOS DOES TEACH

I said previously that *Teach Yourself DOS* does not teach everything there is to know about DOS. But it does try to teach you what you *need* to know. This book prepares you to use DOS in the daily routine operation of your PC.

This book is a self-help DOS tutorial. By explaining concepts and offering exercises that you can run as you read, it enables you to teach yourself DOS. To begin, you will need nothing more than a PC that has DOS installed and a single, blank, formatted floppy diskette. If you do not have these things or do not know whether or not you have them, go to where you bought the PC and tell them what you need. It's a simple request, and they should be willing to comply.

Teach Yourself DOS would have been much easier to write when the PC was first introduced in 1981. DOS was not as complex (or powerful) as it is now, and there were not the varieties of computer configurations that we have today. Because the PC world is more complicated now, PCs and DOS are more difficult to understand, and a need exists for this kind of book — one that retreats to the basics and delivers the primary lessons necessary for a new user to learn DOS.

Turn now to Chapter 1 where you can explore why and how you will Teach Yourself DOS.

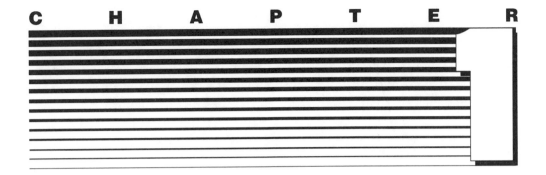

C H A P T E R 1

INTRODUCTION

Who are you? You are a new user of DOS on the family of desktop computing machines called by many names: PC, XT, AT, 386, or Clone. These machines have much in common, but the feature they share that should interest you now is that they all use the Disk Operating System called DOS, MS-DOS, or PC-DOS. Those names are synonymous. From now on, the computer will be referred to as a PC and the operating system as DOS. You are the person charged with getting them to work together.

How did you come to be a new DOS user? Perhaps, like my pal Ron Skipper, you are newly retired and writing your memoirs. Perhaps one day your boss confiscated your typewriter and replaced it with a PC. Or maybe you reported to a new job and found that your duties include using a PC. It could be that PCs have nothing to do with your work but are a newfound hobby. Or maybe you are just trying to keep up with your kids.

Whatever the reason, there you are, facing a keyboard and screen and looking at this most nondescriptive of all user prompts:

C>

or

A>

What do you do next? Read on.

WHY THIS BOOK?

In the Foreword, you learned how a new DOS user found an abundance of advanced DOS reference books. He was not inclined to embark on an extensive study of the subject, preferring instead to learn enough to get on with his writing project. He soon learned that, with the books available, he did not have that choice.

This book, therefore, is about operating DOS well enough to get some work done. You sit at a PC so you can do work, typically running applications such as word processors, spreadsheets, and data bases. While the object of your efforts is the work, the path to that work is by way of DOS, something you need to understand at least well enough to do the work. There is a lot to know about DOS if you want to become a Power User. There is a smaller body of knowledge that is needed to get by. Most of this book is about getting by.

Users

Real users like you use PCs to do work. To do the work, you must run the application programs. To run the applications, you must know how to start them up and how to point them to their respective data (information) files. To run programs and access files, you must understand the mechanism inside the PC that supports those processes. That mechanism is DOS. DOS finds the programs and runs them. DOS finds the data files for the programs and reads from and writes to them. In one way or another, you tell DOS when and how to do these things by issuing commands.

Power Users

Most books about using DOS are aimed at the person who has come to be known as the Power User (PU). The PU is someone who extracts the maximum performance from the PC, using and understanding a complex set of mechanisms including Expanded Memory, memory-resident pop-up utilities, RAM disks, caches, and other DOS-specific features that are unrelated to but support word processing, data base, and spreadsheet applications. PUs can get caught up in the technology. At a cocktail party they will bore you with the various technical aspects of their PCs — their memory size, disk capacity, speed in Megahertz. They do not talk much about the work they do. The medium truly becomes the message.

New Users

Teach Yourself DOS is for the New User (NU). The NU does not want or need to be a PU. The NU does not know what a PU is. The NU wants to get the PC running reliably to get a job done. At a party the NU talks about life.

Many NUs become PUs. All PUs begin as NUs. Whether or not you want to become a PU, *Teach Yourself DOS* is the first step to take in getting what you really need right now — a mastery of the elementary principles of using DOS. In Section II of this book, the parts of DOS that interest the PU are discussed. These commands are not arcane entities that should scare you away, but you can ignore them for now. Later, when you are a seasoned NU, on the brink of PU-hood, you will find good use for them. But from now on and until you get into Section II, there are no further distinctions between New and Power Users. There is just you.

SOME ASSUMPTIONS

So you want to teach yourself DOS? Well, to get started you need a PC that runs DOS. The exercises that you will use to teach yourself require your participation with such a PC. That PC could be configured many ways, and a book such as this one cannot cover every possible configuration. Therefore, certain assumptions are made about your PC.

You Have a Hard Disk Named C

Throughout the lessons and examples in this book, you will see this format:

```
C><something>
```

The C> is the DOS **prompt**, what DOS displays to tell you it is waiting for a command. The <something> is what you type. **Important**: Always assume that you press the **Enter** key (this key is also commonly referred to as the Return key or the key with the big arrow pointing down and to the left) at the end of each command unless you are told otherwise. Pressing the Enter key "executes" a DOS command.

This book uses the C> DOS prompt because it is assumed that you have a hard disk and that the disk drive letter is C. If you do not have a hard disk (a disk physically resident inside your computer), the letter would be A, in which case you would substitute A> wherever you see C>. Disk drive letters and their relation to the prompt will be explained in Chapter 4.

You Have a Floppy Diskette Named A

Many of the exercises use the floppy diskette drive (where you insert a diskette) for you to build examples on. These exercises will frequently use the following format:

```
A><something>
```

Someone Has Installed DOS for You

For you to use DOS, it must be installed. To install DOS, you must understand more about it than you can be expected to understand at first. Therefore, the assumption is that someone has installed it and that when you turn the PC on, DOS is running. Furthermore, the assumption is made that the DOS utility programs are in a place where DOS can find them when you try to execute them. If you are relating this requirement to your installers, tell them that you want the DOS programs to be in the "DOS path," or "DOS subdirectory." This concept will be explained later.

CATCH 22

There is always a catch. You need to understand DOS well enough to set up enough of a system to teach yourself DOS. But, of course, you do not understand DOS that well yet. You will have to trust the instructions given in these exercises to get that preliminary job done for you. Sometimes you will be asked to enter some commands that you have not learned yet. The purpose for those requests will be to help you establish an environment that supports the current exercise. In those cases, you will be asked to blindly follow the instructions. You will learn the reasons later. Such preparatory chores are referred to as "housekeeping."

GETTING OUT OF THE SHELL

When you turn the PC on, you might see a screen that is similar to Figure 1.1. This is the DOS 4.0 Shell. If you see this screen, press F3 to go to the

DOS command line. The Shell is supposed to make things easier. It does, but first you need to learn DOS from the more primitive view of the **command line** (where you see the C> or A> prompt). Why? First, not all DOS commands are available from the Shell. Second, some day you might find yourself at a PC that has an earlier version of DOS and no helpful Shell. You need to understand the command line. Third, the command-line syntax is the basis for all of the DOS features. It came first. The Shell and all other similar menu programs came later.

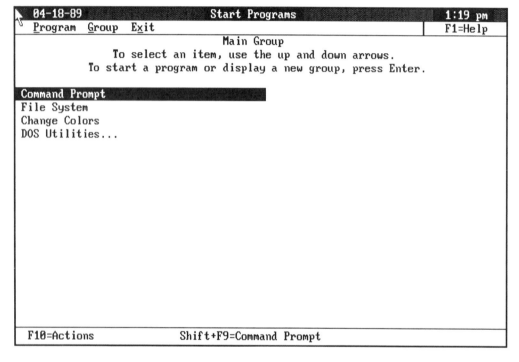

Figure 1.1   The DOS 4.0 Shell

Perhaps your PC was installed with a different shell or menu program. One such program is the Norton Commander. Others are available from commercial, public domain, and shareware sources. Many system installers install their own custom menu programs. If you are using such a program, find out how to get out of it and do so. If you can locate the system installers, have them disable it. You might want it later, but you do not want it getting in the way when you teach yourself DOS. Once you know DOS well enough, you may never again need or want such a shell. Then again, you might prefer it. The use of a shell is a personal choice, and you should not let the opinions of others dissuade you from using one if you like it. But for now, you want to learn grass roots DOS, and that implies an understanding of the DOS command line.

GETTING IN COMMAND

When computer technology was young, the disciplines of computer operation were exercised exclusively by computer programmers and computer operators. The programmers designed the operator "interface" (how programs appear to or communicate with the user) to be a concise and cryptic command language. The reasons for this design are found in the complex nature of the behemoth computers of yore and in the expense of their operation. They were capable of highly complex tasks, and they cost a lot of money to run. The languages were just as complex and consisted of short cryptic sequences of commands. The brevity of these operations kept operator time at a minimum and therefore reduced manpower and processor costs. At least that was the idea.

General users (e.g., office workers) did not operate the computers in those days. They provided input data (usually on paper) and received printed output reports, delivered from the computer room by hand.

As desktop computers began to appear, some of this cryptic command mentality came with them. This circumstance was due to the fact that the first microcomputer programmers were immigrants from the world of the big computers, and big computers were all they knew. This influence is seen even today in the DOS command line.

Other computers, such as the Macintosh, have taken other directions to provide more symbolic and, their creators claim, more intuitive command languages. In a similar vein, there are the DOS shell programs mentioned previously that attempt to make the use of DOS easier by providing menus and pictorial representations of the file structures. But while we inherited the cryptic command methods from the old computers, we inherited as well their main advantage: a concise command language that, once learned, is the fastest and most efficient way to use DOS.

It is often argued that lay users should not be required to learn a cryptic command language. That argument had validity in the days when there was no standard for such a language. The PC, by virtue of its overwhelming acceptance by users of small computers, has become the *de facto* standard desktop computer. On its coattails rides DOS, the *de facto* standard operating system. There is no good reason not to learn DOS if you are going to have computers as a part of your life. And to learn DOS is to learn its command-line conventions.

Once you know DOS from the command-line perspective, you are in command.

THE HELPFUL COMMAND-LINE PROMPT

When you exit the Shell or menu program or start up DOS, you might see a command-line prompt that looks something like this:

```
C:\>
```

or this:

```
C:\DOS>
```

Some well-intentioned person has installed the system to tell you something you are not ready for. Turn off the unwanted help by typing this command immediately following whatever prompt you see (remember to press the Enter key after typing in the command):

```
prompt
```

The prompt that follows is what you want to see each time you enter a session of *Teach Yourself DOS*:

```
C>
```

The reason for disabling the helpful prompt is so that your PC behaves as much like the examples in this book as possible. Later, you will learn how to turn that feature back on, and you can decide if you want to keep it or not.

THE TUTORIAL OBJECTIVE OF TEACH YOURSELF DOS

Teach Yourself DOS uses a structured tutorial approach to its lessons. The objective is to introduce new material at the point where you are ready to learn it. For this reason except for a brief listing in the Appendix, you will not find the DOS commands listed in alphabetical order or arranged functionally. (If you know the name of a command and want to find the exercises that explain it, look in the index.) The material in this book is presented in the order in which you should learn it. Each lesson progresses assuming you have learned the lessons that precede it.

Through the exercises, you will build and change a diskette that will be called the *TYD Learning Diskette*. You must follow the exercises in the order in which they are presented so that the diskette is always set up the way the next exercise expects it.

Often you will learn a concept that is not complete. A Power User might look at a lesson and conclude that the book is flawed because it does not tell the whole truth at that point. This is done on purpose. Many aspects of DOS require circular understanding. You must understand subject C to understand subject B, which requires an understanding of subject A, which cannot possibly be explained until subject C is understood. Such is the nature of complex systems. For this reason, the first explanation of subject A may be incomplete because you have not learned subject C yet. Subject A is revisited when the lessons of subject C are complete. Of such is the structure of a good tutorial.

Call for Help

From time to time you will be asked to make sure of something that you might not be equipped to know. For example, in Chapter 3, you are advised to determine if your diskette drive is high or low density. You are told that if you cannot figure it out for yourself, you should ask someone. This is a common piece of advice, and unless you live in a Tibetan monastery, you should be able to find a nearby PC expert. Other PC users like to be helpful, if only to display their knowledge. Just be careful not to let their enthusiasm get in your way. They might start modifying your system, installing all kinds of stuff—such as menu shells—that will confuse your objective, which is to teach yourself DOS with a minimum of fuss.

Find a friendly fellow user who knows more than you and who does not mind answering a question from time to time.

When and Why?

Tutorials have a responsibility to the student. It is not enough to teach you how something works. A good tutorial should tell you why and under what circumstances you would want to use that something. For example, you might see this command:

```
C>dir t*.*
```

Then you might be told that the command will display a directory of all files that start with the letter "t." Left with that, you might well ask, "So, what?" and never know why you would need to do such a silly thing. Therefore, where it is appropriate and possible in these lessons, you will be given examples of when and why you might use the DOS features being taught.

Tests, Midterms, and Finals

These lessons and exercises have no tests or questions for you to answer. The exercises all have their results fully displayed and explained when the exercise is presented. You should run each exercise on your PC to see that the results are correct, to get practice, and to gain experience and confidence with DOS. But you need not fear the end of the chapter, anticipating a test of your knowledge. You will not find one. If you are motivated to learn DOS, that is enough.

Examples and Experience

This tutorial approach lets you learn by example and, more important, by doing. You need a PC to learn these lessons because you are going to run the exercises, and they involve operating the PC with DOS. You do not learn to fly an airplane, deliver a baby, or cook a chicken by reading a book. You learn by doing. There are books that explain the basics, but you will never know how those procedures work until you use them. We are born knowing how to do some things. Running DOS is not one of them.

SIDE TRIPS

Frequently, the lessons will include some ancillary information, information that is of interest but not essential to the lesson at hand. That information will be presented in the format shown here:

> You can bypass the related information shown in this manner. You will not miss anything needed for the current lesson. The information supports and perhaps explains further some concept under discussion, but if you are in a hurry or otherwise not interested in subordinate knowledge, you can skip the side trip without fear of losing valuable data. These side trips are never used as the only place to present essential information.

FINDING YOUR WAY AROUND

Chapter 11 is special, and you might want to turn to it now to see what it holds; you will certainly use it from time to time. You do not need to wait until you get through the other chapters to use Chapter 11. Whenever you learn a new and complex tool, you might have some idea about what it is going to do for you, but you don't know how. One of the things missing from most introductory books on computer subjects is a subjective index that helps you find the procedure you need, based on an explanation of your problem.

Suppose, for a simple example, you want to see the names of all your word processing document files and you do not know the name or purpose for the DIR command. An alphabetic index of command names is not going to help because you do not know what you are looking for. Finding the DIR command does not help when you do not know that the DIR command is what you want.

You could read the descriptions of all the commands and hope to stumble across the one you want. But many of your tasks on the PC will involve a sequence of commands, and no list will help you find that. Chapter 11 has a set of frequently needed operations. It points you to the exercises that will teach you how to perform the operations. Whenever you find yourself asking, "How do I do thus and so?" turn to Chapter 11 to see if "thus and so" is in there.

GETTING STARTED

Proceed to Chapter 2 and begin your excursion into the fascinating and rewarding realm of DOS. You are ready to begin to teach yourself DOS.

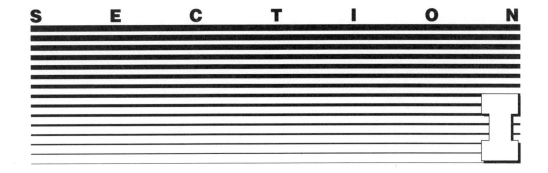

S E C T I O N

THE NEW DOS USER

By now you are probably anxious to begin punching keys. This section, then, is for you, and soon you will be running the exercises that let you teach yourself DOS. Chapter 2 begins this section and has no real exercises, but it is necessary because it explains some of the basics. Chapter 3 explains the differences between diskette formats. When you get into Chapter 4, the exercises and the real fun begin.

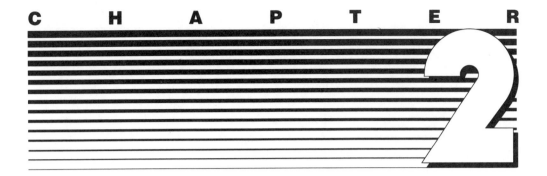

C H A P T E R

2

WHAT IS DOS?

If you are going to teach yourself DOS, you need to know just what DOS is and what its component parts do for you. You will soon realize that DOS is just another computer program, although an important one.

What you will learn in this chapter:

- The purpose of DOS
- What a file is
- How files are named

- What a program is
- What a DOS command is
- The DOS directory structure

THE PURPOSE OF DOS

When you use a PC or any other kind of computer, you run computer programs. Computer programs are sequences of instructions that tell the computer how to do something, and they are created by people called computer programmers. A computer program is usually stored on disk, waiting for you to run it. Then the program is loaded into the computer's main memory to be executed (or run).

DOS is the master computer program that manages the files on the disk file system and runs programs when you ask it to. The phrase "manages the files" means that DOS will create new files, read them, change them, copy them, and delete them whenever it is instructed to do so by you or one of your applications programs (e.g., a word processing or spreadsheet program).

The DOS command line is on the screen at the place where the C> prompt and the cursor appear. As long as no applications programs are running, DOS is waiting for a command. Eventually, you type a command onto the DOS command line, and DOS does something. That action could be something as simple as showing you the current time. Or it could be something as complex as running programs to post a year's worth of general ledger journal entries, print a report of the sales year to date, and schedule an oil change for the company car.

DOS provides a common interface between the user and the PC for the execution of programs. Because there is a DOS, applications programs have a common way to get loaded into memory and executed.

DOS provides a common interface between the programs (e.g., the Word-Perfect program) and the data files (e.g., a letter you wrote in WordPerfect) that are stored on disk. Because there is a DOS, each application program does not have to contain the code (computer commands) that keeps track of where the data files get stored and how they get found, read, written, and deleted.

By working in a DOS-supported environment, there is a measure of compatibility among PCs. Disk data files and programs that work on one PC will work on another because the PCs use the same DOS, and DOS is the proprietor of standard formats for data files and programs among PCs.

LOADING DOS

When you first turn on the PC, it runs a program that is permanently stored in the PC's memory. That program is called BIOS, and it is always there, whether or not you have any disks loaded and even when the power is turned off. BIOS does many things to support the PC's operations, but you need to know only that, upon startup, BIOS automatically looks for the PC's master computer program, the program called the Disk Operating System, or DOS. That's right, DOS is a computer program just like WordPerfect, Lotus 1-2-3, and dBASE IV are computer programs.

When the PC is powered up, BIOS locates DOS on the primary disk medium, which is the hard disk if you have one. If you do not have a hard disk or if a diskette is inserted in the A diskette drive, BIOS looks to the A drive for DOS. BIOS reads DOS into memory and executes the DOS program. After that, DOS takes care of executing all the other programs.

DOS is called the master program because it is the vehicle with which you run other programs. There are utility programs that come with DOS and applications programs that you get from other places. They all run under the DOS umbrella. They will all be referred to as applications programs for now.

When DOS loads, it may display many different messages on the screen, depending on how DOS has been configured by the installer. Eventually though, when the loading is done, DOS will display its command-line prompt, which again looks something like this,

        C>

with the **cursor** (a blinking underline character) just to the right of the greater than (>) character. The cursor indicates where you can begin typing in commands or text.

FILES AND COMMANDS

In the view of the user, DOS's main purpose is to keep track of data files and execute user commands. There is a common thread that runs between files and commands. To understand commands, you need to know how the files are organized and named. To organize and name files, you need to understand the commands that achieve those purposes. You need to understand both to understand either one. To further confuse you, it will be revealed that many commands are programs and all programs are disk files. Let's take it slowly, one step at a time.

FILES

The concept of "files" is an important one. The contents of a DOS disk are organized into files. Everything is in a file. Your word processing documents are files. Your spreadsheets and data bases are files. The programs that comprise the word processing, spreadsheet, and data base software systems are files. DOS itself is stored on the disk in files.

The floppy diskette that you hold in your hand and the hard disk that spins inside the cabinet of your PC can both contain files – lots of files. There is no architectural difference between the two media. The floppy diskette does not have the capacity of the hard disk, but the floppy diskette is removable while the hard disk is not. Other than those two differences, everything you will learn about disks and their files applies equally to floppy diskettes and hard disks.

Perhaps a metaphor would help. Think of your PC as a file cabinet. Think of each hard disk drive or floppy diskette as a drawer in a file cabinet capable of holding many file folders. Each disk file is a file folder. Think of the data records in the disk files as letters, documents, and forms in the file folders. The big difference between the file cabinet and our metaphorical disk filing system is this: you can walk over to the file cabinet, pull anything out, and look at it all by yourself; you cannot see or use the files and records on the disk without the cooperation of the PC, DOS, and your applications programs.

File Names

Every file has a file name. Later you will learn the significance of the unique properties of file names. For now it is enough to know that a file name has this format:

```
<name>.<extension>
```

The < name > is from one to eight characters. The < extension > is optional, but if it exists it has from one to three characters. Typical file names are as follows:

```
LETTERS.TXT
WP.EXE
AUTOEXEC.BAT
```

You name many of the files. Others are named for you by the developers of the applications software you purchase. Still others are named by IBM or Microsoft and are included when you purchase DOS itself.

File names can consist of letters, numbers, and some special characters. The letters are case-insensitive; that is, if you create a file as LETTERS.TXT, you can refer to it later as letters.txt. You could even mix cases, as in LeTTeRs.TxT, but that would make no sense.

Coming Up with a File Name

Do not worry about your responsibility for naming files. There is nothing mysterious or cryptic about the process. A letter to Aunt Milly composed in your word processor might be named MILLY.LTR. You could as easily name it FERN.DOC or BLITZ.FRP. DOS would not care. You would care later, however, when you looked at those meaningless file names and wondered what on earth was in the files with the funny names. Try to select names that reflect the purposes of the files. On second thought, do worry some about this — it's worth the time to get it right.

File Name Extension Conventions

Remember that file names consist of a name and an extension. The name can be up to eight characters long, and the extension can be up to three characters long. The name and extension are separated by a period, like this:

```
NAME.EXT
```

The name part usually identifies the particular file. The extension usually identifies a category of files. For example, files with the extension of .DOC might be word processing documents. This would be a convention that you would choose.

There are conventions that specify certain defined extensions to some file names. DOS has its conventions, and they must be complied with by those who develop applications programs. Many applications programs also impose file-naming conventions, usually allowing you to pick a file name to be combined with a defined extension. Others leave you all the latitude you want. Following are some examples. These three-character extensions are some of those used by DOS. (Each of these extensions and their purposes will be discussed soon.)

- .EXE — an executable program
- .COM — an executable program
- .BAT — a batch command file
- .SYS — a DOS device driver program (mostly)

You could use these extensions for your own file names. But you should know how DOS will deal with files that have these extensions in their names, and you should avoid their use to avoid confusing your files with files that have a defined purpose in the realm of DOS.

With these conventions, you can look at a file's name and know something about the purpose for the file. If you see FOOBAR.BAT, you will say to yourself, "Aha! A batch command file that performs the FOOBAR function (whatever that is)." Eventually you will say those kinds of things to yourself more and more. That's one of the effects of using PCs to any extent. You begin to talk to yourself.

You might consider developing your own file extension conventions. If you named that letter MILLY.LTR, why not name all your letters with the .LTR extension?

Conventions for the File Name

If you write a letter to Aunt Milly every month, you might name them MILLY01.LTR in January, MILLY02.LTR in February, etc. When January rolls around again, you'll need to either move those files somewhere else to reuse the file name MILLY01.LTR or use a different convention.

Later, when file name wild cards are discussed, you will see how helpful such practices can be.

File Types

There are three basic kinds of disk files:

- data files
- program files
- subdirectory files

Data Files

These files are just what you would expect. They contain records of data that are created, retrieved, and modified by applications programs. They take many forms and have many different functions.

A word processor will have a number of different data files. The ones you will be most familiar with are the letters and documents that you type. But others are equally as important. There are printer definition files that specify the characteristics of the printer you have chosen. (Printers are so different that it takes a complex file of configuration statements to describe the way the printer works to the program.) There are font files that let you use many different character formats in your publications. These files don't change often, and you can usually disregard them, taking their presence for granted.

Other applications programs will have their own data files. For example, an accounts receivable system will have a file of vendors, a file of invoices, and a file of payments.

Most applications programs have configuration data files that describe the unique way you want them to run. You may be able to select screen colors, custom keystrokes, and functional options. DOS itself has several such configuration data files.

Many applications programs use files of help text to give you helpful information while you are running the program.

These are just some of the different kinds of data files that a DOS system manages for its applications programs. There are many more. But to DOS, they all look the same. A program can create them, read them, update them, and delete them, and DOS provides the means to do that. What the applications program does with them beyond that is its business and yours, and DOS does not care.

Program Files   There are four kinds of programs that are stored in disk files. Two of them are functionally identical and one of them is not for you, the user, to worry about at first. But you need to know about all of them so that you will recognize them when you see them. Soon you will see how programs are executed from the command line. For now, consider how DOS stores programs in disk files.

When you purchase a software package, it comes on a diskette. That diskette has files that comprise the software package. You already learned what some of the data files are. The other files comprise the software program.

Software programs are stored in files with these file name extensions:

.EXE
.COM
.BAT
.SYS

Those are the four kinds of programs. They were mentioned earlier. The .EXE and .COM files are the same as far as you are concerned. There are technical differences that programmers know about, but to the user, they are the same. If, for example, you see the file named

WP.EXE, you may assume that the file is a program that you can run.

The .SYS file is a DOS device driver program. You do not run this program yourself. DOS runs it when you turn the PC's power on. If you add an applications program or a hardware device (such as a mouse) to your system, you might need to install a .SYS file into DOS. There is a special file named CONFIG.SYS that is not itself a device driver program but that figures prominently in the installation of other .SYS files. The CONFIG.SYS file will be discussed later in the book.

Subdirectory files   The third kind of disk file is the subdirectory. You'll learn just what a subdirectory is later in this chapter.

COMMANDS

A command is something you type when the video cursor is at the screen command line. To execute the command, you type its name, perhaps some **parameters** (extra optional instructions), and press the Enter key. Then the command performs some action.

Commands can be one of three general types: internal DOS commands, program file commands, and batch file commands. To you they all look alike. To DOS they work differently. Eventually you will need to know this difference to know how and when you can use the different types of commands.

Internal DOS Commands

In Chapter 4 you will begin to execute commands in earnest. But you can try one now. Type in this command, pressing the Enter key at the end (do *not* type the C> prompt; that is what should appear on the screen):

```
C>time
```

DOS tells you what time the PC thinks it is and asks you to enter a new setting for the clock. You can press the Enter key if you do not want to change the time. The TIME command is an example of an internal DOS command. The command is built into DOS and there does not need to be a disk file with the .COM, .EXE, or .BAT extension to execute the command.

Now enter this command:

```
C>dir
```

What you see will depend on how your computer is set up, but whatever it is, take note. This command is probably the most frequently used of the internal DOS commands. It is the Directory command, which displays a directory of disk files. There are several variations on this command, and you will learn to use them all.

Program File Commands

You run a program by typing its name on the command line. For example, to run a program named FOO.EXE or one named FOO.COM, you would type this command:

```
C>FOO
```

Program file commands are found in files with the .COM and .EXE extensions. To execute these commands, DOS must be able to find the file. For example, you could type this command on the command line:

```
C>hello
```

If DOS finds a file named HELLO.COM or HELLO.EXE, DOS will read that file into memory and execute the program that is stored in the file. When the program finishes, it returns control to DOS at the command line.

Batch File Commands

Batch file commands are found in files with the .BAT extension. A batch file is a file of text that you can prepare with a text editor program or with some word processors. The text in the file contains commands that DOS recognizes just as if you typed them yourself on the command line.

If, in the example just given for program file commands, DOS did not find HELLO.COM or HELLO.EXE, then DOS would look for a file named HELLO.BAT. If DOS finds that file, DOS reads the file one line at a time and executes the commands in the file. The .BAT file is a batch file that contains a series of DOS commands. Later you will learn about batch files. For now, you need to know that if you see a file with the extension .BAT, it is like a program to you, and you can execute it just as you can the .EXE and .COM files.

.COM, .EXE, and .BAT files differ in one important way. DOS assigns them a precedence. You can have three files with the same file name but with these three extensions. For example, you can have FOO.COM, FOO.EXE, and FOO.BAT. If you attempt to run FOO, DOS will take the .COM file over the .EXE and .BAT files. If there is no .COM file, the .EXE file takes precedence. Note that giving command files similar names like this is not a good practice and is seldom if ever done intentionally.

Batch files provide a way for you to put frequently used sequences of commands into a procedure that is executed with just one command name. You can put a complex series of commands into a named batch file and execute all those commands by typing the batch file's name.

Chapter 9 contains details about how you build batch files.

Invalid Commands

A fourth kind of command is the invalid one. If you type a command that DOS does not recognize, DOS will display this message:

```
Bad command or file name
```

That message means that DOS does not recognize the command as being one of its internal ones and cannot find a matching .COM, .EXE, or .BAT file to load and execute. Try it now. Type any string of nonsense and press the Enter key.

THE DOS DIRECTORY STRUCTURE

By now you know that DOS keeps files on disks. Up to now all you've done is learn the different kinds of files. But it was suggested that DOS manages those files by allowing you and your programs to create them, get at them, change them, and get rid of them. The analogy of a file cabinet was used, comparing the PC to the cabinet and the disk to the drawer full of files. But the analogy goes deeper. With the high capacity of the hard disk, it is possible to have so many files that you cannot keep track of them. You need a filing system that lets you organize your files into functional separators, or groups of related files.

The PC can handle a lot of different applications, albeit one at a time. You can have many different kinds of files in there. Segmenting the file folders into functional groups will make things easier to find.

If all your worldly possessions are in a pile on the garage floor, you will have trouble finding your socks each morning. That's why you have a drawer for socks in the bedroom and another one in the kitchen for silverware. We naturally organize our possessions into a functional hierarchy that makes them easier to find. Birds do it, bees do it, most people do it, and PC users should do it too. Consider the chaos that would result if you began moving your personal possessions around willy-nilly.

DOS provides a hierarchical structure of directories and subdirectories into which you can store files. You design the hierarchy and DOS manages it under your direction. Every disk starts life with nothing on it. Someone must prepare it for use by DOS. You'll learn how to prepare a disk later with the FORMAT command, but for now assume that it has been done. A formatted disk has the beginnings of a hierarchical directory structure with the top of the hierarchy, which is called the "root directory." What goes below that is up to you, and Figure 2.1 shows a typical PC hierarchical disk directory structure.

```
\ ................................. (Root Directory)
├─ command.com
├─ autoexec.bat
├─ WORDPROC  ...................... (Word Processing)
│       ├─ SOFTWARE .................. (Word Processing Software)
│       │       └─ wp.bat
│       └─ DOCS ..................... (Word Processing Documents)
│               ├─ LETTERS .............. (Letters)
│               │       ├─ milly01.ltr
│               │       └─ milly02.ltr
│               └─ MANUSCRP ............. (Manuscripts)
│                       └─ novel.doc
├─ SPRDSHT ....................... (Spreadsheets)
│       ├─ SOFTWARE .................. (Spreadsheet Software)
│       │       └─ ss.bat
│       └─ SHEETS ................... (Spreadsheet data files)
│               └─ taxes88.sps
└─ DOS ........................... (DOS Utility Programs)
        ├─ backup.com
        ├─ chkdsk.com
        └─ etc.
```

Figure 2.1   Typical DOS directory structure

Figure 2.1 is a pictured representation of a directory structure. Such a structure will figure significantly in the lessons that follow.

SUMMARY

You should now understand the basic ideas behind these subjects:

- what DOS is and how it is loaded

- how DOS manages files, runs programs, and provides the command-line user interface

- what a DOS file is

- file names and file naming conventions

- the file types: data, program, and subdirectory

- DOS internal commands

- command files

- DOS subdirectories

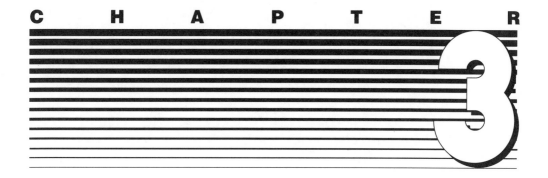

C H A P T E R

3

DISKETTES

This chapter is devoted to diskettes because there are so many different kinds, and you need to know what kind you have so you can get on with the lessons. This book assumes that you have at least one floppy diskette drive in your PC.

What you will learn in this chapter:

- The sizes of diskettes
- The five diskette capacities
- Compatibility issues
- What the FORMAT command is

Many PCs have diskette drives only. A diskette drive accepts a floppy diskette, which can be removed and replaced with another floppy diskette at any time. Many other PCs have hard disk drives, which cannot be removed and which have a higher capacity than floppy diskettes. Usually a PC with a hard disk has one or two diskette drives as well. Rarely does a PC have a hard drive and no diskette drives at all. Most commercial software is distributed on floppy diskettes, and you will need a diskette drive to install such software onto your hard disk.

A diskette stores information when the diskette drive "writes" streams of magnetic impulses on the diskette's surface. To retrieve the information, the disk drive "reads" those streams of information back into the computer's memory. The disk drive performs the read and write operations at the direction of the currently running computer program, perhaps as a direct result of a command you have issued.

There is a category of PC called the "diskless work station," which has no disk drives at all, but which is connected to a local area network where some other PC, called a "file server," has all the disk power for everyone on the network.

THE HISTORY OF THE DISKETTE

In the early seventies, IBM invented the diskette as a portable medium for small-scale data storage. The first diskette was 8" wide, about the size of a 45 RPM record. It was a paper disk coated with a magnetic emulsion. The disk was sealed inside a square paper envelope with apertures to expose the recording surface. Early home computers used this 8" diskette as their primary mass storage device.

In the late seventies, well before the introduction of the IBM PC, diskette manufacturers designed a smaller diskette, one that was 5 1/4" wide. This diskette became the standard for the IBM PC in 1981, and, as a result, a standard for practically everyone else.

A third physical diskette design came into acceptance with the introduction of the laptop PC compatibles. This diskette is 3 1/2" wide, and its protecting envelope is made of rigid plastic with a sliding metal shield that protects the recording surface when the diskette is out of the drive. It is the handiest of the diskettes because it is the most durable and because it fits neatly into your shirt pocket, which is its finest attribute.

Most PC/XT/AT computers support the 5 1/4" diskette size. Most laptop computers and PS/2s support the 3 1/2" diskette size. The 8" diskette is all but extinct.

Figure 3.1 shows the two kinds of diskettes found in most PCs.

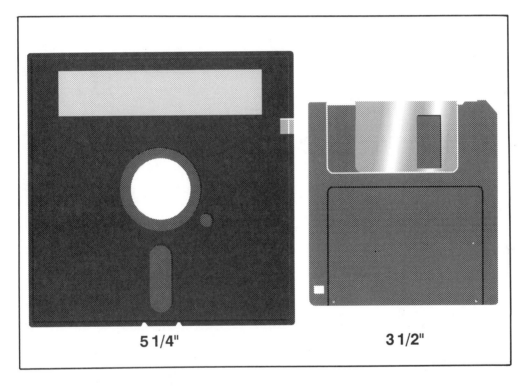

Figure 3.1   The two diskette sizes

DISKETTE CAPACITIES

The two diskette sizes come in five different capacities. A diskette's storage capacity, or memory, is expressed in characters, also called "bytes." The standard units of measure are K bytes where K is equal to 1024 bytes and M bytes where M is equal to 1024K. The notations for these measures are KB and MB. This shorthand is used for convenience.

It would be better if novice users could be spared such technical jargon, but these expressions are common and necessary if you want to converse intelligently with your fellow users. Besides, you will need to know these terms in order to talk to the sales person where you will buy your diskettes. Computer sales people do not know much English.

The 5 1/4" Diskettes

The 5 1/4" diskettes are found in three sizes: 160KB, 360KB, and 1.2MB.

160KB:
Single-sided

The first PC came with a diskette drive that recorded on one side of the 5 1/4" diskette. These diskettes had a capacity for 160K bytes of storage. The very first version of DOS, version 1.0, which is seldom used anymore, supported this 160KB format only. You will rarely find this format being used today, although the newer 5 1/4" drives can read from and write to the older diskettes. You can ignore this format from here on.

360KB:
Double-sided-
double-density

With DOS 2.0 came support for diskette drives that can read from and write to both sides of a 5 1/4" floppy diskette. This format provides for 360KB capacity. To be used in this format, a diskette must have been manufactured to meet the specifications that will support it. Most 5 1/4" diskettes that you buy today will support the 360KB format.

1.2MB:
High-density

When the IBM AT was introduced, a new format for diskettes came with it—the high-density 1.2MB drive. This format has been a pain to most users because of the incompatibility problems it presents, and IBM omits reference to it in their DOS 4.0 documentation, allowing the 360KB format to be the standard for 5 1/4" diskettes. Nonetheless, many PC clones still come equipped with 1.2MB drives. To use a 1.2MB drive in its high-density mode, you must use diskettes that are rated for high-density storage.

If you do not know whether your 5 1/4" drive is rated for 1.2MB or only 360KB, you must find out. When IBM introduced the drive, they stamped its cover with an identifying logo, but few of the clone drive makers followed that convention. If you have a high-density diskette and your drive will read it, then you know you have a high-density drive. Without that clue, you will have to ask someone to help you figure it out.

The 3 1/2" Diskettes

The 3 1/2" diskettes are found in two sizes: 720KB, and 1.44MB.

720KB

DOS 3.2 offered support for the 720KB 3 1/2" diskette, although many laptop computers support this format with earlier DOS versions.

1.44KB

DOS 3.3 added support for the 1.44MB 3 1/2" diskette format. As with the 1.2 MB 5 1/4" drive, the only way to know if your PC's disk drive supports the larger format is to try to have your drive read a 1.44KB diskette.

DISKETTE COMPATIBILITY

There are compatibility concerns with the various disk formats. Because the purpose of this book is to allow you to teach yourself enough DOS to get some work done, the advice here is to find a format that works for you and get on with it. Later, when you become a power user, you can try mixing and matching disks with the drives. To guide you, here are the basic rules of compatibility (and incompatibility) among the disk formats.

- Obviously, you cannot put a 3 1/2" diskette into a 5 1/4" drive.

- Equally as obvious, you cannot put a 5 1/4" diskette into a 3 1/2" drive.

- You can read from and write to 720KB diskettes in both formats of 3 1/2" disk drives. You can read from and write to a 1.44MB diskette only in a 3 1/2" drive that is rated for 1.44MB diskettes.

- You can read from and write to 360KB diskettes in both formats of 5 1/4" disk drives. 360KB diskettes that have been written to on a 1.2MB disk drive may not be readable on 360KB disk drives. This is not a fixed rule, but it happens often enough that you should never depend on being able to freely move data between the two drive formats without some difficulty.

- You can read from and write to a 1.2MB diskette only in a 5 1/4" drive that is rated for 1.2MB diskettes.

Figure 3.2 illustrates the operational relationships between the different formats of disk drives and diskettes. First, find out what type of diskette drive you have and locate it in the top portion of the diagram. Then look below your drive type for check marks that indicate which type of diskettes it can read from and write to.

Disk Drive Type							
5.25 ″				3.5 ″			
360KB		1.2MB		720KB		1.44MB	
Read	Write	Read	Write	Read	Write	Read	Write
√	√	√	√*				
		√	√				
				√	√	√	√
						√	√

(Left row labels: DISKETTE — 5.25″ 360KB, 1.2MB; 3.5″ 720KB, 1.44MB)

* 360KB diskettes written by 1.2MB drives might not be readable by 360KB drives.

Figure 3.2   The relationship between diskettes and disk drives

PREPARING A DISKETTE FOR OPERATION (FORMAT)

When you buy a box of diskettes, they do not come ready to use. You must prepare them for use by "formatting" them. The DOS FORMAT command manages this task. First, you must know which diskette format you have. Then you must run the DOS FORMAT command, which is described in an exercise in Chapter 4. There are a number of ways to format a diskette, but for these lessons you will use the FORMAT command that formats the diskette in its "default" configuration (i.e., the specifications already set up by DOS).

The FORMAT command differs among different versions of DOS. When you get to the FORMAT exercise in Chapter 4, be sure you know the kind of disk drive you have and the version of DOS you are running. Be sure, also, to have a blank diskette of the proper type for the exercise.

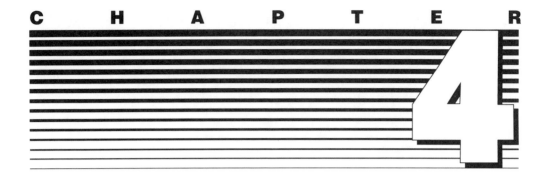

C H A P T E R

4

INTRODUCTION TO DOS COMMANDS

This chapter is your first step in learning and using DOS. First, some basic DOS commands will be discussed. Then, to ease the process, you are going to make a special learning diskette. This diskette will figure prominently in the lessons that follow. As you get farther into the lessons, you will add features to the diskette. You must start with a blank diskette, and your PC must have DOS installed, as assumed in the first two chapters.

What you will learn in this chapter:

- The DOS command-line edit keys
- Clearing the screen
- Viewing the DOS version
- Logging onto a different disk drive
- Setting the clock/calendar
- Formatting a floppy diskette
- File names and wild cards

- Disk directory displays
- Copying a file
- Deleting a file
- Renaming a file
- Adding, deleting, and changing to a subdirectory
- Viewing the subdirectory tree
- Disk volumes and labels

GETTING STARTED

Turn on your PC now and allow it to load DOS. You should now be looking at the ominous DOS prompt:

```
C>   or   A>
```

From this point, you enter DOS commands. The cursor is positioned to the right of the prompt, and DOS is waiting for you to type a command. The area of the screen from where the cursor is to the right margin is the DOS command line. Actually, the command line is longer than that, but you will rarely if ever get much past the center of the screen when entering commands.

The command line can be on any line of the screen. Its position is determined by where the prompt is displayed.

DOS EDIT KEYS

As the DOS commands are discussed, you will be trying them on your PC. You will be told to type a command, and you should then type it and press the Enter key. Of course, you might make some mistakes, and DOS has some ways to let you correct your mistakes. Certain keys have editing properties when you are typing onto the DOS command line.

These edit keys are not only for correcting mistakes. You can use them to speed up certain repetitive operations that involve sequences of similar commands.

The Backspace Keys

Suppose you want to use the DIR command as discussed in Chapter 2. But suppose you make a keying error and enter DOR instead of DIR. Type that error now, but do *not* press the Enter key.

```
C>dor
```

Either the large Backspace key just above the Enter key or the left arrow key on the numeric keypad will move the cursor back one position, erasing the character it covers.

You can press the Backspace key twice and see this display:

```
C>d
```

Now type the "ir" and press Enter. The DIR command is executed.

This method is more useful for longer commands. Many programs require sets of parameters on the command line following the command's name. Using the Backspace key is a handy way to correct a keying error at the time you make it.

The Escape Key

Suppose you type in a command and realize that you do not want to execute it. If you make that realization before pressing the Enter key, you can press the Esc key to cancel the command. Try that now. Type the DIR command followed by the Esc key instead of the Enter key.

```
C>dir          (Press Esc key.)
```

DOS will display a slash (\) character and will move the cursor down one line as shown here:

```
C>dir\
    _                ←(The cursor is here.)
```

You may now enter any other command you want after the backslash, and whatever you typed before the backslash will be ignored. If you don't want to enter another command, simply press Enter and the DOS prompt will reappear.

The F3 Key

Suppose you want to repeat a command. The F3 key will display the most recently entered command on the command line, with the cursor at the end of the command, waiting for you to press the Enter key. You can press the Enter key, or you can use the Backspace key to edit and change the command. Try this now. Type the DIR command. (Press the Enter key at the end of the command.)

```
C>dir
```

You will see a file directory on the screen. Press the F3 key. You will see the DIR command repeated as shown here:

```
C>dir_   ←  (The cursor is at the end of the command.)
```

Press the Enter key. The DIR command is repeated.

The F1 Key and Forward Arrow Key

Just as the F3 key repeats the previous command, so do the F1 key and the forward arrow key on the numeric keypad, except these keys repeat the command one character at a time. Try this now. You just executed the DIR command in the last exercise. Press the F1 key once. You will see the first letter (d) of the DIR command as shown here:

```
C>d_     ←  (The cursor is just past the d.)
```

Press the F1 key a second time. Now the second letter (i) is displayed:

```
C>di_
```

Press the F1 key a third time and the entire DIR command is displayed. You can now press the Enter key to execute the command.

Any Displayable Key

While you are pressing the F1 key to space forward through the previous command, you can press any key that will display on the screen. The value of that key will replace the keystroke that was in that position in the previous command. Try this after having executed the DIR command. Press the F1 key once. You will see the first letter (d) of the DIR command as shown here:

```
C>d_
```
← (The cursor is just past the d.)

Now type the "e" key and see this display:

```
C>de_
```

Press F1 again, and the "r" from the DIR command is displayed as shown here:

```
C>der_
```

Of course, DER is not a command, and if you press the Enter key now you will get this message:

```
Bad command or file name
```

Instead, you can press the Esc key to ignore the command.

The Ins Key

While using the F1 key, you can press the Ins (for Insert) key before typing other characters. Then the characters you type are inserted into the previous command rather than overwriting the character that was in that position. Try this now. First execute the DIR command to get a command to repeat. Then press the F1 key once. You will see the first letter (d) of the DIR command.

```
C>d_                    ←  (The  cursor  is  just  past  the  d.)
```

Now press the Ins key and type the characters "espa" as in the following:

```
C>despa_
```

Now press the F1 key twice, and you should see this word:

```
C>despair_
```

The first "d" and the last "ir" are from the previous DIR command. The others were typed by you. DESPAIR is not a DOS command, but do not despair. Press the Esc key to reject it. Then press the Enter key to get the DOS prompt back.

The Del Key

When using the F1 key to repeat a command, you can alter that command by using the Del key to delete characters from the previous command. This requires that you remember what the previous command is. Try this. Execute the DIR command again. Then press the F1 key once. You will see the first letter (d) of the DIR command:

```
c>d_
```
← (The cursor is just past the d.)

Now press the Del key followed by the F1 key. The Del key deletes the "i" of the DIR command, so you will see this display:

```
c>dr_
```

Press the Esc key to get rid of the invalid DR command.

Mixing the Keys

You can mix all of these keys in building a new command from an old one. Do not expect to fully understand how you will use these features until you are into the more complex DOS commands and the commands in your applications programs. But put a marker in this section of the book and return to this discussion later. The study of DOS often requires that you learn a subject to get to the next plateau, yet the full power of the subject will often not be apparent until several plateaus later.

CLEARING THE SCREEN

The CLS command is the second of the internal DOS commands that you will learn. Remember from Chapter 2 that internal DOS commands are ones that are built into DOS. You do not need a program file to execute them.

Try clearing the screen. Enter this command:

```
C>cls
```

The screen goes blank, and the DOS prompt and cursor are in the upper left corner of the screen.

Why would you clear the screen? Sometimes, it just gets cluttered. Other times you do not want anyone to see what you have been doing. You may want to display something—a directory perhaps—so you can print the screen, and you do not want the residue of earlier operations to appear on the screen print. (Screen printing is discussed later in this chapter.)

THE DOS VERSION

Currently, there are eight versions of DOS: 2.0, 2.1, 2.11, 3.0, 3.1, 3.2, 3.3, and 4.0. When the PC was first introduced, there was a DOS version 1.0. It is incompatible in many ways with the versions that followed and is rarely used. A new version number indicates that some improvements and/or changes were made to DOS by its developers.

You can see what version you have by entering the VER command like this:

```
C>ver
```

The VER command tells you the DOS version with a message similar to the following:

```
IBM Personal Computer DOS Version 3.30
```

The message may vary depending on where you got the DOS program. It might say MS-DOS, and it might include the name of a particular computer manufacturer. But the relevant information is the DOS version number. Regardless of the other information, all versions 2.0 are functionally identical and all versions 2.1 are identical, and so on.

Why should you care about the version? Often an applications program specifies that it will run with a particular version of DOS or higher. You need to know if you have a compatible DOS version to know if you can run that program.

THE CALENDAR AND CLOCK

DOS keeps track of the current date and time. When first loaded, DOS does not know the date and time and must be told. If you have an AT-class machine or if your PC/XT has a clock/calendar card installed, there is hardware that remembers the date and time in your PC, and the startup procedures set the current date and time into DOS's clock and calendar. If, however, you are using a PC/XT without a clock/calendar board, then you must set the date and time each time DOS is reloaded. If you fail to do so, DOS thinks it is midnight on January 1, 1980 every time you reload DOS.

> If you fail to keep your date and time set properly, DOS will associate incorrect dates and times with the files that it creates for you. Not only will this cause confusion when you attempt to manage your own files, but the DOS procedures for backing up and restoring files will not always work properly. The BACKUP and RESTORE commands are discussed in Chapter 7.

DOS contains user commands to read and set the date and time. They are named, naturally enough, DATE and TIME. Try these commands now. Type this command:

```
C>time
```

DOS will display the time in this manner:

```
Current time is 7:30:22.75p
Enter new time:
```

If you do not want to change the clock, press the Enter key. To change the time, you must use military time, where the hour is 0 to 23. Just enter the time in minutes and seconds as in the following example:

```
19:30
```

To view the date, type this command:

```
C>date
```

DOS will display the date in this manner:

```
Current date is Tue 04-18-1989
Enter new date (mm-dd-yy):
```

If you do not want to change the date, press the Enter key. To change the date, enter it in the format shown here:

```
06-24-89
```

You can use a shorthand version of either command to set the date or time without the prompting displays. Simply include the new date or time on the command line, as shown here:

```
C>date 06-24-89
C>time 19:30
```

If the date and time in your hardware clock is wrong, the DATE and TIME commands do not reset them. DATE and TIME only modify DOS's copies of the date and time. These are not permanent copies but remain in effect only until the next reload of DOS (after you turn your computer off and then back on, for example).

The procedures for resetting the hardware date and time vary from machine to machine. The IBM AT comes with a program called SETUP that includes a procedure to reset the clock and calendar hardware. Many clones use the same kind of approach. The IBM SETUP program itself works with most clones. Clock/calendar add-on boards for the PC/XT use other programs to change the settings, and there is no standard program.

You will need to change the clock at least twice a year when daylight savings time comes and goes.

LOGGING ONTO A DIFFERENT DISK DRIVE

Up until now, you have used the C> prompt in all the examples and exercises. The letter C is the standard designation for the default hard disk on most PCs. Remember that you were advised to substitute the A> prompt in the example commands if your PC does not have a hard disk.

When you issue commands, these commands are usually effective relative to the drive that is shown in the prompt. This drive is called the "currently logged-on drive." For example, when you issue the DIR command from the C> prompt, you will see a directory of files that are stored on the C drive. If you were to issue that command from the A> prompt, you would see a directory of the files on the A drive.

You can change the currently logged-on drive with a simple DOS command. For now, put any diskette you might have handy into the A drive and enter this command:

    C>A:

You will now see this prompt:

    A>

Issue the DIR command now, and you will see a directory of the files on the diskette that you inserted in the A drive. Put a different diskette in the A drive and enter the DIR command, and you will see a different directory.

To return to the C drive, issue this command:

    A>C:

You will see this prompt once again:

    C>

This is an important lesson. Unless something in the command explicitly refers to a different drive, the command is generally assumed to be directed to files on the currently logged-on drive.

Of course, there are exceptions and other ways to override this rule, and you will learn them in time, but for now make sure you understand this concept well: Unless DOS is told otherwise, all commands relate to the currently logged-on disk drive, which is reflected in the prompt you see on the screen (e.g., C>).

FORMATTING A FLOPPY DISKETTE (FORMAT)

In Chapter 3, you learned about the differences between the various kinds of floppy diskettes and disk drives, and you learned that you must use the DOS FORMAT command to prepare a diskette for use. Now, you will build your learning diskette by using the FORMAT command. Enter this command at the DOS command line:

```
C>format a: /s
```

You have told DOS to format a diskette in the A drive and to write a copy of DOS onto the diskette. When this operation is complete, you will be able to start up your PC with the diskette in the A drive. DOS will be on the diskette, and the system will be able to "boot" itself from that DOS image.

> The terms "boot" and "reboot" mean to load DOS into memory and get it running. It is a programmer's nickname for the earlier expression to "bootstrap," which, no doubt, refers to a machine's metaphorical ability to pull itself up by its own bootstraps. The term originated in the 1950s when computers were new.

When you issue the FORMAT command as shown earlier, DOS responds with the following message (or a similar message, based on what version of DOS you are using):

```
Insert new diskette for drive A:
and strike ENTER when ready...
```

While DOS is formatting the disk, it will give you a running status. DOS 3.3 shows this message:

```
Head    0 Cylinder   0
```

The head and cylinder numbers change to show you how far the FORMAT command has progressed on the diskette. The maximum numbers vary depending on the kind of diskette you are formatting. DOS 4.0 displays the percentage of the diskette that has been formatted.

When the FORMAT command is done, it displays information similar to the following:

```
Format Complete
System transferred
   1213952 bytes total disk space
     78336 bytes used by system
   1135616 bytes available on disk
Format another (Y/N)?
```

Type "n" followed by the Enter key. The numbers in the display will vary depending on the version of DOS and the kind of diskette you are formatting.

The FORMAT command you just issued has two command-line **parameters**, the a: and the /s. Command-line parameters appear on the command line after the command name. They provide additional information to tell the command how to execute. In this case, the a: parameter tells the FORMAT command to format the diskette in the A drive, and the /s parameter tells the FORMAT command to add a copy of DOS to the diskette.

Note: to format a diskette without a copy of DOS being transferred, omit the /s parameter in the FORMAT command. This is the more usual way to format a diskette. You do not often need a copy of DOS on your diskettes if you have a hard disk.

Chapter 7 has exercises to teach you the advanced FORMAT options. For now, you know all that most users will ever need to know about the FORMAT command.

SOME LESSON REVIEW

You have just begun building your learning diskette by running the FORMAT command. That's a big step. You have actually made your PC do something meaningful. Put a label on the diskette that says "TYD Learning Diskette" so you'll be able to find it the next time you want it. Put it back into the A drive. Now you can run some exercises that will review some of the earlier lessons you learned.

Reloading DOS

Remember that DOS will reload itself from the diskette in the A drive if one is there. You have one there now, so try it. Hold down the Ctrl and Alt keys while simultaneously pressing the Del key. This is the famous DOS three-fingered salute. You'll use it a lot.

The PC will beep and grind and eventually read DOS from the diskette you just built. PCs can be set up a number of different ways, so this new boot operation may differ from the one you are accustomed to seeing. But you can expect that DOS will now load and will automatically run the DATE command and then the TIME command. Press the Enter key for each command, as shown here:

```
Current date is Tue 04-18-1989
Enter new date (mm-dd-yy):     ← (Press Enter.)
Current time is 7:30:22.75p
Enter new time:                ← (Press Enter again.)
```

Now DOS will display its prompt like this:

```
A>
```

Because you loaded DOS from the A drive, A is automatically the currently logged-on drive. Note that none of the startup options (such as running a DOS Shell menu program) that were installed in your computer are in effect because you are booting from a sterile, unprepared system diskette, the one you just built. Gradually, you will build up that diskette's functionality. For now, it will serve your purposes just as it is.

The DIR Command

The DIR command will now show you what is in the root directory of your TYD Learning Diskette. Type the following command:

```
A>dir
```

DOS will give you a display like the one shown here:

```
Volume in drive A has no label
Directory of A:\

COMMAND  COM    25307    3-17-87  12:00p
         1 File(s)   1135616 bytes free
```

This display tells you that the diskette has no label (more about labels later) and has one visible file in its root directory, a file named COMMAND.COM. The size of the file and the date and time of its creation follow. The last line tells how many bytes of memory are free on the diskette. Note that the number of free bytes matches the number displayed when you ran the FORMAT command. You will see a different number, depending on the version of DOS and the kind of diskette you use. This example was made with a 1.2MB diskette and DOS 3.3.

The sum of the number of bytes free and the size of COMMAND.COM does not equal the 1.2MB capacity of the diskette. This is primarily because DOS includes two other files that are hidden from you. A hidden file is not shown by the DIR command. The hidden files are the 78336 bytes assigned to the system when you issued the FORMAT /S command earlier.

Changing the Logged-On Drive

If your computer has a hard disk, change the currently logged-on drive to that of the hard disk, like this:

```
A>c:
```

Now you are logged onto the C drive, and the prompt appears like this:

```
C>
```

If you use the DIR command, you will see the files in the root directory of the C drive. That may or may not be what you saw earlier when you used the DIR command for the C drive. What you saw then would depend on how your initialization procedures were installed. You might have been looking at the contents of a subdirectory. You will learn what that means soon.

While you are logged onto the C drive, you can still look at a directory of the A drive if you want. Try this now. Enter the following command:

```
C>dir a:
```

You will see the same directory you saw when you were logged onto the A drive. The DIR command allows you to specify a different drive on the command line.

This is an important addition to your knowledge. The DIR command can be expanded by the use of command-line parameters. You will learn more of them soon.

AN INTRODUCTION TO AUTOEXEC.BAT

Why did DOS ask for the date and time when you loaded it from your TYD Learning Diskette? It probably does not do that when you load DOS the way it was installed on your hard disk.

When DOS is loaded, it looks for a file named AUTOEXEC.BAT in the root directory (the term "root directory" is explained later) of the boot disk. If it does not find that file, DOS assumes that you need to set the date and time. If it does find the AUTOEXEC.BAT file, DOS assumes that if you need to manually set the date and time, the AUTOEXEC.BAT file will take care of it.

> The AUTOEXEC.BAT file is a file of text that contains DOS commands. These commands are automatically executed every time DOS is loaded. That's how the file got its name. There is a lot more to know about AUTOEXEC.BAT, but you do not need to know that information just yet. You will learn more about AUTOEXEC.BAT in later chapters.

For now, you will build yourself an AUTOEXEC.BAT file on the TYD Learning Diskette so that DOS will load without troubling you about the date and time ever again. AUTOEXEC.BAT is introduced here for the reason just given and also to show you how to add a file to the diskette. You need some files on the diskette so that you can run some more exercises.

USING COPY TO BUILD A FILE

The simplest way to get a file onto the TYD Learning Diskette is with the DOS COPY command. This is a housekeeping chore that supports the lessons.

COPY is the DOS command that lets you copy files. It has many variations on its command format, and you will learn them soon enough. Right now, you will learn what is needed to add a file to the TYD Learning Diskette.

The COPY command format follows this pattern:

```
COPY <source> <destination>
```

Generally, you use file names and/or disk drives for the source and destination of the COPY command. But you can also use fixed device names to copy from the keyboard or to the screen or printer. When the COPY command is addressed in detail, you will see how that works. For now, you will copy some text from the keyboard to a file on the TYD Learning Diskette. Specifically, you will build the first version of the AUTOEXEC.BAT file. Log onto the A drive with this command:

```
C>A:
```

Next, enter the command shown here:

```
A>copy con autoexec.bat
```

With that command you said, effectively, "copy con, the source, to autoexec.bat, the destination."

You have told DOS that you want to copy whatever is typed at the console keyboard ("con" means "console" to DOS) into a file named AUTOEXEC.BAT.

> Using COPY to build a file from the keyboard is not the way COPY is normally used. COPY is most often used for copying disk files from one place to another, perhaps to write a file that is on a hard disk to a diskette. This unconventional introduction to COPY is for convenience so that you can build files to use in the lessons. The COPY command receives a more comprehensive treatment later in this chapter.

Because you are logged onto the A drive, the AUTOEXEC.BAT file will be written to the A drive by the COPY command. After you enter the COPY command just shown, the cursor moves to the screen line below the command, and DOS waits for you to type something. Type the following lines very carefully. Press the Enter key at the end of each line. Before you press the Enter key, you can use the Backspace key to correct any typographical errors on the line.

```
echo off
cls
echo Teach Yourself DOS Learning Diskette
ver
```

After the last line is typed, press the F6 key and then press Enter. The F6 key tells DOS that you are done typing. The diskette drive will grind away as the file is written, and then you will see the DOS A> prompt once more.

The AUTOEXEC.BAT file you just created contains two commands you already learned, CLS and VER. The other command, ECHO, is unfamiliar. ECHO is a special DOS batch command. You rarely use it anywhere except in a batch (.BAT) file. The first use of ECHO, the one that says "echo off," tells DOS not to display the other commands in the batch file while they are being executed. The second ECHO command tells DOS to display the text on the ECHO command line when the ECHO command is encountered. This command provides a way for you to display meaningful messages while a batch file is processed. Chapter 9 describes batch files and their use.

Give the three-fingered salute (simultaneously press Ctrl-Alt-Del). After some wheezing and grinding from the disk drive, your screen will contain this display:

```
Teach Yourself DOS Learning Diskette

IBM Personal Computer DOS Version 3.30

A>
```

(Your version number might be different, of course, from the one in the previous display.)

Note that you have now loaded DOS without being pestered to enter the date and time. The mere presence of the AUTOEXEC.BAT file suppresses those prompts. If your PC has no hardware clock/calendar, you can include the DATE and TIME commands in the AUTOEXEC.BAT file. These commands would then at least insure that you do not ignore the need for the correct date and time when DOS is loaded.

Now try the DIR command:

```
A>dir
```

You will see the display shown here. Note that the AUTOEXEC.BAT file
is now on the diskette.

```
COMMAND  COM   25307   3-17-87  12:00p
AUTOEXEC BAT      63   4-20-89  10:00a
        2 File(s)   1135104 bytes free
```

With the addition of AUTOEXEC.BAT, the number of
bytes free on the diskette has been reduced. Oddly, the
reduction is greater than the size of AUTOEXEC.BAT.
In fact, although AUTOEXEC.BAT is only 63 bytes long,
the number of bytes free is now 512 bytes less than it was
before AUTOEXEC.BAT was added to the diskette.
This is because DOS allocates disk storage space in even
blocks. On a 1.2MB diskette, the blocks are 512 bytes
each. A 360KB diskette uses 1024-byte blocks. Most
hard disks use blocks of 2048 bytes.

The blocks that DOS allocates to files are called
"clusters." On the 1.2MB diskette, files with lengths from
1 to 512 bytes use one cluster; files from 513 to 1024 bytes
use two clusters; and so on in increments of 512.

TYPING A FILE

DOS has an internal command named TYPE that lets you display the
contents of a text file. You can use this command to view the
AUTOEXEC.BAT file that you just created. Enter this command:

```
A>type autoexec.bat
```

DOS will now "type" the contents of the file on the screen. This is what you will see:

```
echo off
cls
echo Teach Yourself DOS Learning Diskette
ver

A>
```

Look familiar? It's what you built earlier with the COPY command. The TYPE command is an example of a command that requires a command-line parameter, in this case the name of the file to be typed.

Many DOS and applications program commands require file names on the command line, and there are different ways that you can specify these file names, depending on the command's requirements. Some commands operate on one or more files, and there are ways to use the DOS file name convention to specify a group of files rather than just one. In addition, you can specify files that are on other disk drives. The next exercise shows how.

FILES ON OTHER DRIVES

Remember how you used the DIR command to look at the directory of a different drive. You issued the following command to view the A drive's directory while you were logged onto the C drive:

```
C>dir a:
```

Commands that take file names as parameters can also have disk drive designators that tell DOS to look somewhere other than the currently logged-on drive. To illustrate that concept, log onto the C drive like this:

```
A>c:
```

Then use the TYPE command that you just learned to type the AUTOEXEC.BAT file, which you know to be on the A drive, like this:

```
C>type a:autoexec.bat
```

The display is the same as shown in the previous exercise because the AUTOEXEC.BAT file is the same one. Even though you are logged onto the C drive, you can access files on other drives. Notice the a: before the file name. That is a drive designator, and it tells DOS to find the file on the A drive.

Remember that unless told otherwise, DOS expects files named on the command line to be in the default drive (i.e., the drive indicated by the currently displayed prompt). The previous command shows how DOS is told otherwise. If you leave out the optional disk drive designator, DOS looks to the default drive. If you include it, DOS looks to the drive that is specified in the command.

Now log onto the A drive once more to learn about file names that specify groups of files rather than just one file:

```
C>a:
```

FILE NAMES AND WILD CARDS

Up until now, you have used unambiguous file names, or file names that completely specify the file in question. When you specified AUTOEXEC.BAT, you gave the full name of the file, and there was no question about what file you meant. There are occasions when you want to name a group of files. The most frequent use of this operation is in the COPY command, which you will learn more about later. But it is frequently used in the DIR command, too. You will now learn about how to specify an ambiguous file name.

First, however, for these exercises you will need more files on the TYD Learning Diskette, and so some housekeeping is in order. Build the first of the example files with this command:

```
A>copy con autotype.bat
```

Type the following lines, pressing Enter at the end of each one:

```
cls
echo Running AUTOTYPE.BAT
```

Press F6 and then press Enter. DOS will tell you one file was copied. This file is a batch file that you could run by entering the command AUTOTYPE. You do not need to do that just yet. Build the next file with this command:

```
A>copy con charley.001
```

Type the following line, again pressing Enter at the end:

```
This is CHARLEY.001
```

Press F6 and then press Enter. DOS will tell you one file was copied. This file is just a file of text. Build the last file with this command:

```
A>copy con charley.002
```

Type the following line and then press Enter:

```
This is CHARLEY.002
```

Press the F6 key and then Enter again. DOS will tell you one file was copied. You have just added three files named AUTOTYPE.BAT, CHARLEY.001, and CHARLEY.002 to the TYD Learning Diskette. Use the DIR command to verify that the files were added:

```
A>dir
```

You will see this display:

```
COMMAND   COM   25307   3-17-87   12:00p
AUTOEXEC  BAT      63   4-20-89   10:00a
AUTOTYPE  BAT      32   4-21-89    9:00a
CHARLEY   001      12   4-21-89    9:00a
CHARLEY   002      21   4-21-89    9:00a

      5 File(s)   1133568 bytes free
```

The dates and times will be different, of course, and the bytes free will be different if you are using anything other than a 1.2MB diskette.

Now that you have that housekeeping chore out of the way, you can learn about **wild cards**.

When you specify a file name on the command line, you can do so in such a way that you have specified a set of files rather than just one individual file. You do this by inserting wild cards in the file name. Now look at the simplest variation of this concept.

The Asterisk (*) Wild Card

The asterisk character in a file name is a wild card. It represents all occurrences of file names that share certain characteristics. For example, if you say *.BAT, you are requesting all files that have the extension .BAT regardless of their names. Try it now. Enter

```
A>dir *.bat
```

This is what you will see:

```
AUTOEXEC BAT      63    4-20-89   10:00a
AUTOTYPE BAT      32    4-21-89    9:00a

      2 File(s)   1133568 bytes free
```

The asterisk wild card works in file name extensions as well. Enter this command:

```
A>dir charley.*
```

This is what you will see:

```
CHARLEY   001       21    4-21-89    9:00a
CHARLEY   002       21    4-21-89    9:00a

          2 File(s)   1133568 bytes free
```

You asked for a directory of all files that were named CHARLEY, regardless of their extensions.

It will not surprise you then that you can use the asterisk on both sides of the period. For the DIR command, using *.* will deliver the same directory as specifying no file name at all. This is because *.* is a **global** designation and means all file names regardless of extension and all extensions regardless of file names, and, of course, that specification specifies all file names.

The asterisk can also be used to specify part of a file name. You can give the part of the file name you know and use the asterisk to select the rest of it. For example, try any of these commands:

```
A>dir a*.*
A>dir au*.*
A>dir aut*.*
A>dir auto*.*
```

This is what you will see:

```
AUTOEXEC BAT       63    4-20-89    10:00a
AUTOTYPE BAT       32    4-21-89     9:00a

          2 File(s)   1133568 bytes free
```

Try this command:

```
A>dir c*.*
```

You will see this display showing all the files that begin with the letter C:

```
COMMAND  COM    25307    3-17-87   12:00p
CHARLEY  001       21    4-21-89    9:00a
CHARLEY  002       21    4-21-89    9:00a

    3 File(s)   1133568 bytes free
```

The asterisk can be used the same way in the file name extension.

You might use partial file names when you cannot completely remember the name of the file you are looking for. Suppose you know that you named all your Appendix files App-*something*, but you do not remember the details of the second part. You could use this command:

```
A>dir app*.*
```

The Question Mark (?) Wild Card

The question mark is a wild card specifier that you substitute for a single character of the file name.

For example, to see all the files that have a zero as the second character of the file name extension, enter this command:

```
A>dir *.?0?
```

This is what you will see:

```
CHARLEY  001      21   4-21-89   9:00a
CHARLEY  002      21   4-21-89   9:00a

       2 File(s)   1133568 bytes free
```

The asterisk matches all file names, and the ?0? mask matches the extensions that have any character as the first character, a zero as the second, and any character as the third.

Not all commands work with wild cards. Some commands, by virtue of what they do, operate with only one file. TYPE is an example of such a command. If you use a wild card in the file name for TYPE, it will display the first file that matches the file name specification.

> Many applications programs do not work with wild cards in their file specifications. You must determine from the program's instructions whether wild cards are allowed.

DELETING A FILE (DEL)

Sometimes you will want to delete a file. The file might be an old one, an earlier version of something you have updated, or just something you want to get rid of to make room on the disk. The DEL command is used for that purpose. You can use wild cards in the DEL command. The AUTOTYPE.BAT, CHARLEY.001, and CHARLEY.002 files on the TYD Learning Diskette have served their purpose, so you can delete them. Enter these commands.

```
A>del autotype.bat
A>del charley.*
```

Use the DIR command to see that the files have been deleted. You will learn more about the DEL command when you have learned about DOS subdirectories.

SUBDIRECTORIES

In Chapter 2, the concept of DOS subdirectories was explained. The DOS file system can be organized into a hierarchy of subdirectories. You saw a typical subdirectory structure in Figure 2.1. Figure 4.1 shows the structure you will build on the TYD Learning Diskette. Each subdirectory has a name. The directory at the top of the hierarchy is called the "root" directory and has the peculiar name of "\" (backslash). That directory is the only one in the hierarchy that has a fixed name. All the subdirectories below the root are named by you when you create them. A subdirectory can contain files, and it can contain other subdirectories. In Figure 4.1, the root directory contains the files named COMMAND.COM and AUTOEXEC.BAT, and the subdirectories are named WORDPROC, SPRDSHT, and DOS. WORDPROC contains the subdirectories named SOFTWARE and DOCS. SPRDSHT contains SOFTWARE and SHEETS. The DOCS subdirectory under WORDPROC contains LETTERS and MANUSCRP subdirectories. For clarity in Figure 4.1, the names of subdirectories are in capital letters, and the names of files are in lowercase.

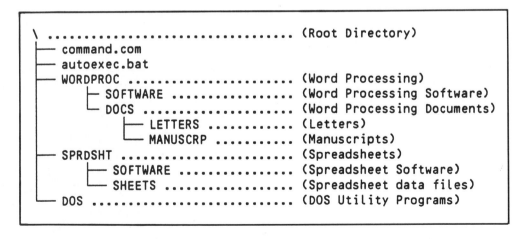

Figure 4.1   The TYD Learning Diskette with subdirectories you will build

Consider the words "directory" and "subdirectory." The root directory, WORDPROC, SPRDSHT, and DOS are all directories. So are the subdirectories under WORDPROC and SPRDSHT. The root directory, however, is not a subdirectory because it is not subordinate to a higher directory. All other directories are subdirectories, being subordinate either to the root or to another subdirectory. The generic term "subdirectory" will be used unless the root directory is being referred to, in which case "root directory" will be used.

> To further confuse matters, the display from the DIR command will be called a "directory." So, when you use the DIR command, you are getting a directory of a directory — or of a subdirectory. Try not to let these naming conventions get to you. That's how the DOS designers set it up when they created DOS. Eventually, these apparent ambiguities will become part of your lexicon, and the nonsense will seem natural.

There are three subdirectory operations to learn. You can make (or create) a subdirectory, remove a subdirectory, and change to a different subdirectory.

The Currently Logged-On Subdirectory

Up until now, you have stayed in the root directory of the TYD Learning Diskette and the C drive. You have logged onto first one drive and then the other, but you have ignored subdirectories because you have not learned them yet.

Look again at Figure 4.1. Just as you can be logged onto a drive, you can be logged onto one of the subdirectories of the currently logged-on drive. When you start out, you are logged onto the root directory, which is named \ (backslash). You can change the logged-on directory with the CD command, which will be discussed shortly. What are the implications?

When you change disk drives, all commands refer to the newly logged-on disk unless you specify otherwise. The same rule applies to subdirectories:

When you change subdirectories, your commands will apply to the most current subdirectory unless you specify otherwise.

Before you can play with subdirectories, you must create some on the TYD Learning Diskette. To do that, you use the MD command.

Making a Subdirectory (MD)

You make a subdirectory with the MD command, which has the following format:

```
A>md <subdirectory path>
```

The < subdirectory path > parameter specifies the subdirectory. The **path** consists of the names of the subdirectories separated by backslashes. The root directory is named backslash, too, which tends to confuse the learning process but is a disguised blessing — it makes things easier after you get used to it. Make some subdirectories now. You will use the structure shown in Figure 4.1 for the exercise.

Begin with this command:

```
A>md \wordproc
```

You have told DOS to make a subdirectory named WORDPROC under (or subordinate to) the root directory. Subdirectory paths are specified with the topmost directory at the beginning, and the root directory (\) is the topmost directory. To verify that the subdirectory was made, use the DIR command:

```
A>dir
```

In addition to the other files on the TYD Learning Diskette, you will see this entry:

```
WORDPROC      <DIR>        4-22-89    8:45a
```

The < DIR > token tells you that WORDPROC is a subdirectory file.

Note that there are two more subdirectories immediately under the root directory in Figure 4.1. These are named SPRDSHT and DOS. Make those subdirectories now:

```
A>md \sprdsht
A>md \dos
```

Use the DIR command to see that the subdirectories were made.

The WORDPROC subdirectory has two subdirectories named SOFTWARE and DOCS. Make those subdirectories by specifying the full path to them. Enter these commands:

```
A>md \wordproc\software
A>md \wordproc\docs
```

Note that the path specification uses the backslash to separate the names of subdirectories. The first backslash is, however, the name of the root directory and, because it is a backslash, does not need another separator. It makes no sense when it is explained, but it makes sense when you look at a path specification.

The \WORDPROC\DOCS subdirectory has two subdirectories named LETTERS and MANUSCRP. Make them now with these commands:

```
A>md \wordproc\docs\letters
A>md \wordproc\docs\manuscrp
```

The SPRDSHT subdirectory has two subdirectories named SOFTWARE and SHEETS. Make those subdirectories by specifying the full path to them. Enter these commands:

```
A>md \sprdsht\software
A>md \sprdsht\sheets
```

The TYD Learning Diskette is now complete as far as its directory structure is concerned, and its structure should resemble the structure in Figure 4.1. This diskette will be the basis for the exercises throughout most of the rest of the book. You will add and remove subdirectories and files as you need them to make the points under discussion. But the diskette, as it appears now, is the foundation.

Using a Subdirectory Path in a Command

As a preliminary exercise in the use of subdirectories, look at how they might affect the DIR command. Enter this command:

```
A>dir \wordproc
```

You will see this display:

```
Volume in drive A has no label
Directory of A:\WORDPROC

.               <DIR>       4-22-89    8:45a
..              <DIR>       4-22-89    8:45a
SOFTWARE        <DIR>       4-22-89   10:24a
DOCS            <DIR>       4-22-89   10:24a
        4 File(s)    1129984 bytes free
```

This is the directory display of the **WORDPROC** subdirectory. Note that the drive and subdirectory name are shown above the directory display.

The two peculiar files named "." and ".." (dot and dot-dot) are always seen at the top of any subdirectory. Their purpose is to provide internal linkage to the parent directory of the subdirectory; in this case, the parent directory is the root directory. There is no reason that you should see these files other than that a **DOS** designer decided you should. You can generally ignore these entries in a subdirectory.

The other two files are the **SOFTWARE** and **DOCS** subdirectories that you built previously. Enter this command:

```
A>dir \wordproc\docs
```

You will see this display:

```
Volume in drive A has no label
Directory of A:\WORDPROC\DOCS

.              <DIR>         4-22-89    8:45a
..             <DIR>         4-22-89    8:45a
LETTERS        <DIR>         4-22-89   10:24a
MANUSCRPT      <DIR>         4-22-89   10:24a
        4 File(s)    1129984 bytes free
```

Finally, enter this command:

```
A>dir \wordproc\docs\letters
```

You will see this display:

```
Volume in drive A has no label
Directory of A:\WORDPROC\DOCS\LETTERS

.              <DIR>         4-22-89    8:45a
..             <DIR>         4-22-89    8:45a
        2 File(s)    1129984 bytes free
```

This is a display of a subdirectory that has no files (other than the useless dot and dot-dot).

Removing a Subdirectory (RD)

You can remove a subdirectory from a disk if that subdirectory is empty, that is, if it contains no files. First, you will make a dummy subdirectory to use in the exercise. Enter this command:

```
A>md \dummy
```

Next, you will add a subdirectory to the dummy subdirectory. Enter this command:

```
A>md \dummy\dummy01
```

Now, put a file in the \DUMMY\DUMMY01 subdirectory. This is a further example of using subdirectories in the file names of commands. Enter this command:

```
A>copy con \dummy\dummy01\test.txt
```

Note that the path, \DUMMY\DUMMY01, is separated from the file name, TEST.TXT, with a backslash. That is the convention for naming files with their subdirectory names. You'll do more of this soon.

Type some lines of text, pressing Enter at the end of each line:

```
abcdefg
now is the time
whatever you like
```

Press F6 and the Enter key. To verify that the file was built, enter this command:

```
A>dir \dummy\dummy01
```

78

You will see this display:

```
Directory of A:\DUMMY\DUMMY01

.              <DIR>        4-22-89    8:45a
..             <DIR>        4-22-89    8:45a
TEST    TXT       45        4-22-89   10:49a
        3 File(s)    1128448 bytes free
```

Now you have a subdirectory with a file in it. Try to remove the lowest subdirectory. Enter this command:

```
A>rd \dummy\dummy01
```

You will see this display:

```
Invalid path, not directory,
or directory not empty
```

That display is the catch-all error message for any reason why you cannot remove a subdirectory. In this case, the subdirectory is not empty. It has the TEST.TXT file in it. Before you can remove the subdirectory, you must delete the files in it. Enter this command:

```
A>del \dummy\dummy01\test.txt
```

Now the subdirectory is empty, and you can remove it. But before you try to remove \DUMMY\DUMMY01, try to remove \DUMMY. It is a sub-directory, and you should be able to remove it. Enter this command:

```
A>rd \dummy
```

You will get the same catch-all error message. Why? The \DUMMY subdirectory is not empty. It still has the DUMMY01 subdirectory in it, which must be removed before the \DUMMY subdirectory can be removed. Enter this command:

```
A>rd \dummy\dummy01
```

That command worked. Now try the one that did not work before:

```
A>rd \dummy
```

This time the command worked, and the TYD Learning Diskette is back to the subdirectory structure shown in Figure 4.1.

Changing to a Different Subdirectory (CD)

When you first start these sessions, you are logged onto the root directory of the TYD Learning Diskette. Figure 4.2 shows this relationship. You are logged onto the directory named "\" and can view and otherwise access the files named COMMAND.COM, AUTOEXEC.BAT, WORDPROC, SPRDSHT, and DOS. The last three of these files are subdirectories. Note that even though there is nothing in the DOS subdirectory, it is a subdirectory nonetheless.

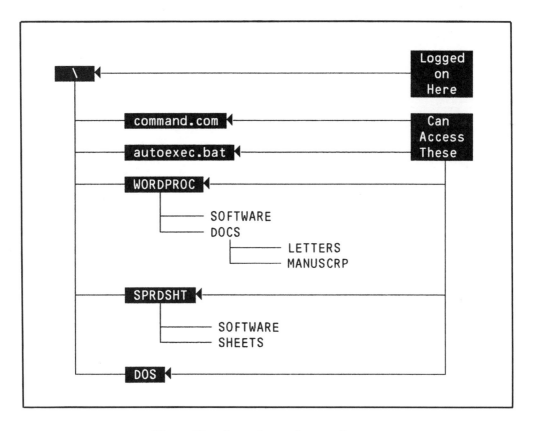

Figure 4.2   Logged onto the root directory

Suppose you want access to the files that are in the **WORDPROC** subdirectory, and you do not want to explicitly identify the subdirectory path every time you name a file. You will need to log onto the **WORDPROC** subdirectory with the CD (Change Directory) command. Enter this command:

```
A>cd \wordproc
```

Figure 4.3 shows how the parameters in the CD command just executed relate to the subdirectory structure. The backslash in the command points to the root directory, and the named subdirectory is WORDPROC.

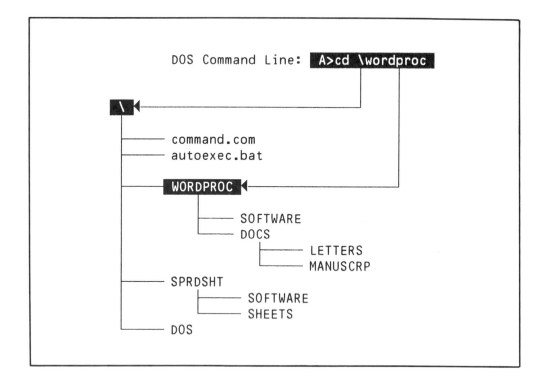

Figure 4.3   Logging onto WORDPROC

Figure 4.4 shows the effect of the CD command just executed. You are now logged onto the WORDPROC subdirectory and have access to the files named SOFTWARE and DOCS. These files are also subdirectories.

Because you have logged onto WORDPROC, you no longer have implicit access to the COMMAND.COM and AUTOEXEC.BAT files in the root directory. You can still get at them by including an explicit path with the file name on the command line, but if you just give the file names, DOS will not know where those files are.

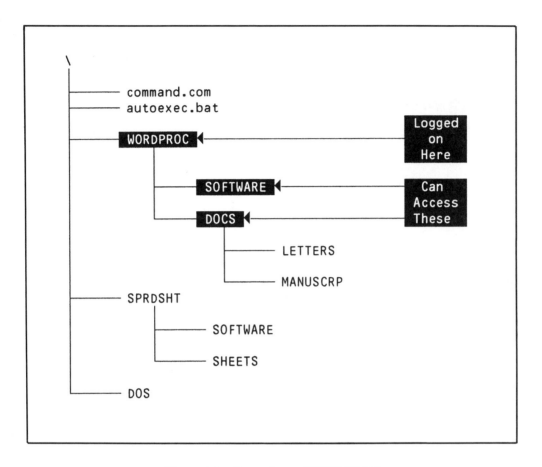

Figure 4.4   Logged onto WORDPROC

Suppose you wanted to be in the **LETTERS** subdirectory below the DOCS subdirectory. You can begin by moving to the DOCS subdirectory as shown in Figure 4.5, but that would be an unnecessary extra step.

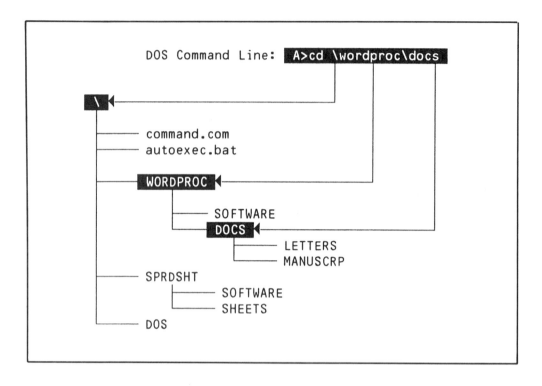

Figure 4.5   Logging onto DOCS

Instead of logging onto DOCS to get to LETTERS, you can log directly onto LETTERS by naming the full path to the subdirectory. Enter this command:

```
A>cd \wordproc\docs\letters
```

Figure 4.6 shows the relationship between the parts of the command-line parameter just used and the TYD Learning Diskette subdirectory structure.

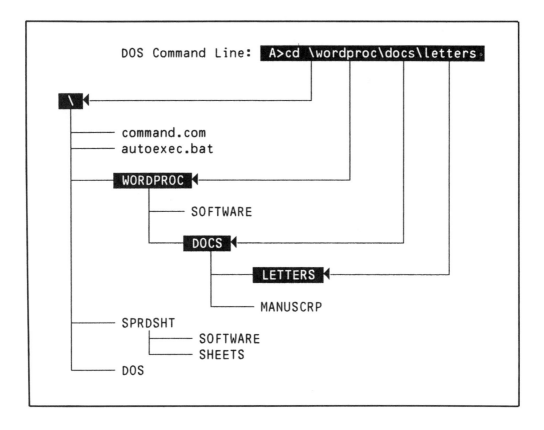

Figure 4.6   Logging onto LETTERS

Figure 4.7 shows the effect of the CD command just executed. You are logged onto the LETTERS subdirectory and have access to any files that might be stored there.

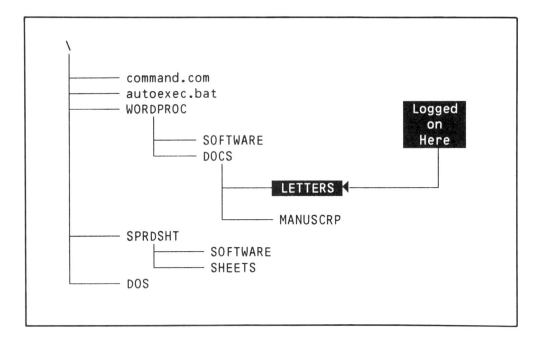

Figure 4.7   Logged onto LETTERS

But now that you are there, you cannot do much because the LETTERS
subdirectory is empty. You need some files in this subdirectory to play with.
Just as before, you will use the COPY command to build a file. Enter this
command:

```
A>copy con milly01.ltr
```

This is your first letter to Aunt Milly. If you had word processing software
on this disk, you could use it to write the letter. But you have not gotten that
far yet. Type some text in the letter to Milly. It does not have to be this text
exactly. Anything will do.

```
April 22, 1989

Dear Aunt Milly,
How are you? Wish you were here.
                    Sincerely yours,
                    Kilgore Trout
```

Press the F6 key and the Enter key.

You need a second letter, and you can use the same technique to write it. Put different text in the second letter so you can tell them apart later. Name the file that contains this letter MILLY02.LTR.

Use the DIR command to see that the two letters are indeed in the \WORDPROC\DOCS\LETTERS subdirectory.

Figure 4.8 shows the TYD Learning Diskette subdirectories and the two files you just added. It shows that you are logged onto LETTERS and that you can access MILLY01.LTR and MILLY02.LTR.

(See Figure 4.8 on next page.)

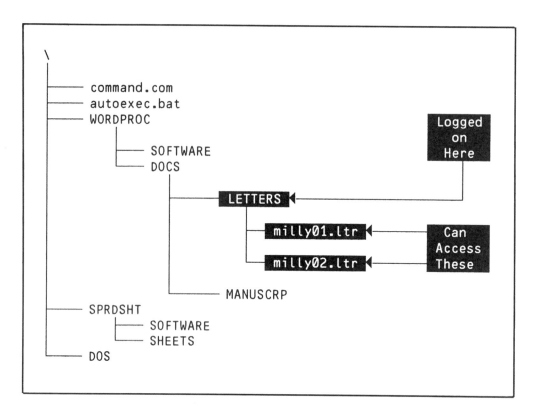

Figure 4.8　　　*Accessing files in LETTERS*

Subdirectory Shortcuts

Earlier you learned that the dot-dot (..) file in every subdirectory is used by DOS to support linkage to the subdirectory's parent directory. That is why the root directory has no dot-dot file; the root has no parent. You can use the dot-dot file as a shortcut to change to the parent of the subdirectory on which you are currently logged.

As of the most recent exercise, you should be logged onto the \WORDPROC\DOCS\LETTERS subdirectory of the TYD Learning Diskette. Enter this command:

```
A>cd ..
```

By changing to the dot-dot subdirectory, you automatically change to the parent of the current subdirectory without needing to remember its name. This last command has logged you onto the \WORDPROC\DOCS subdirectory.

Changing to an Immediately Subordinate Subdirectory

You can change to a subdirectory that is immediately subordinate to the one you are logged onto by specifying its name alone. You are currently at the \WORDPROC\DOCS subdirectory. Enter this command:

```
A>cd manuscrp
```

Note that there are no backslashes or prefix subdirectory names. This command moves you down to the \WORDPROC\DOCS\MANUSCRP subdirectory from the \WORDPROC\DOCS subdirectory. This technique works at any level. You can also use it with additional levels of subdirectories. To see how that works, change to the \WORDPROC subdirectory now with this command:

```
A>cd \wordproc
```

To move down to the MANUSCRP subdirectory at the lowest level in the hierarchy, enter this command:

```
A>cd docs\manuscrp
```

Moving Laterally to Another Subdirectory

You can also use the dot-dot shortcut to move laterally to another subdirectory that is at the same level below the parent as the subdirectory you are now logged onto. From the \WORDPROC\DOCS\MANUSCRP subdirectory, enter this command:

```
A>cd ..\letters
```

This command changes to the \WORDPROC\DOCS\LETTERS subdirectory because \WORDPROC\DOCS is the parent of the MANUSCRP subdirectory you were previously logged onto, and LETTERS is a subdirectory under DOCS.

You are not restricted to moving via dot-dot to a subdirectory that is at the exact same level as where you are logged on. You can move to a subdirectory below a subdirectory at the same level. Just now you are at the subdirectory \WORDPROC\DOCS\LETTERS. Enter this command:

```
A>cd ..\..\software
```

This command changes you to the WORDPROC\SOFTWARE subdirectory. You used two dot-dot names in this command. The first one refers to the DOCS subdirectory, the parent directory of LETTERS, which is where you started from. The second dot-dot refers to WORDPROC, the parent directory of both DOCS and SOFTWARE. Thus, a double dot-dot separated by a backslash refers to the grandparent of the current directory.

Now enter this command:

```
A>cd ..\docs\letters
```

This moves you back to the LETTERS subdirectory, which is a nephew (child of a sibling) of the subdirectory where you started (SOFTWARE).

Changing to a Remote Subdirectory

No matter where you are logged on, you can change to a completely different subdirectory, unrelated to the current one, by using its fully qualified, unambiguous DOS path. Currently, you are logged onto the \WORDPROC\DOCS\MANUSCRP subdirectory. Enter this command:

```
A>cd \sprdsht\sheets
```

This command changes you to the \SPRDSHT\SHEETS subdirectory. By specifying the first backslash, you have fully qualified the subdirectory name.

Changing to the Root Directory

You can change to the root directory while logged anywhere. Enter this command:

```
A>cd \
```

This command logs you onto the root directory of the TYD Learning Diskette.

Displaying the Currently Logged-On Subdirectory

From time to time, you will want to be reminded of where you are logged on. The CD command issued with no parameters will tell you where you are. Try it now. Enter

```
A>cd
```

Because you are logged onto the root directory of the A drive, you will see this display:

```
A:\
```

Change to a lower subdirectory and try the CD command without parameters again.

```
A>cd \wordproc\docs\letters
A>cd
```

You will see this display:

```
A:\WORDPROC\DOCS\LETTERS
```

The PROMPT Command

Some users prefer to see the prompt for the currently logged subdirectory all the time without having to ask for it. You can tell DOS to include the subdirectory as a part of the prompt by issuing the following PROMPT command:

```
A>prompt $p$g
```

The prompt will now always take this form:

```
A:\WORDPROC\DOCS\LETTERS>
```

The $p puts the path designation into the path, and the $g puts in the greater-than (>) sign.

Return to the beginning of the CD exercises and repeat them with the prompt configured this way. You will not, of course, need to rebuild the letters to Aunt Milly. Decide from these exercises whether you prefer the prompt to include the subdirectory path or not. If you do not want to continue with it, you can turn it off by using the PROMPT command with no parameters:

```
A>prompt
```

There are other uses for the PROMPT command. You can make the prompt be anything you like. Enter:

```
A>prompt [HERMAN'S SPIFFY COMPUTER CO]:
```

Your prompt will be whatever you tell it to be. One caution: You cannot use some special characters explicitly in the prompt. Those characters have special meanings on a command line. They are discussed in Chapter 6. The PROMPT command allows you to use the dollar sign as a prefix to substitution characters that put special things in the prompt.

Following is a table of characters that, when prefixed with the dollar sign in a PROMPT command's parameters, will make special substitutions:

The $ Character	The Substitution
$	$
_	Carriage return, line feed
B	|
D	The date (example: Mon 4-24-1989)
E	The ASCII Escape Character
G	>
H	Backspace
L	<
N	The Current Drive
P	The Current Drive and Path
Q	=
T	The time (example: 11:40:25.41)
V	DOS Version

You can use combinations of these characters to make all kinds of interesting prompts to clutter up your command line. If you come up with a prompt display that you want to install permanently, you can put the PROMPT command in the AUTOEXEC.BAT file. Then, whenever DOS is reloaded, your customized DOS prompt will take effect.

It is assumed that you are using the unadorned DOS prompt that you have seen in all the examples so far. To reconfigure your prompt to the default after playing with it, issue the PROMPT command with no parameters.

In Chapter 7, you will learn about the ANSI.SYS console device driver program. There you will learn special PROMPT commands that you can use to control screen colors and other effects.

FILE NAME PATH SPECIFICATIONS

You have learned how to create and move among subdirectories and how to put files in them. Next you will see how commands can cross subdirectory boundaries so that your software can be in one subdirectory and your data files can be in another.

The TYD Learning Diskette is organized so that you will have things related to word processing in the WORDPROC subdirectory. Under the WORDPROC subdirectory, the word processing software will be in the SOFTWARE subdirectory and documents will be in the DOCS subdirectory. The DOCS subdirectory is further divided into the LETTERS and MANUSCRP subdirectories. This subdirectory organization is typical. With such an organization, the software is isolated from your work, and the different aspects of your work—in this case letters and manuscripts—are isolated from one another.

To see how this organization is put into use, you will simulate the presence of some word processing software. First, change to the SOFTWARE subdirectory with this command:

```
A>cd \wordproc\software
```

Next, you will create a file that simulates a word processor. The file will be named WP.BAT and will be a DOS batch file. All this file will do is use the TYPE command to type a document that you specify on the command line. Enter this command:

```
A>copy con wp.bat
```

Now type these lines into WP.BAT:

```
echo off
cls
echo WP: -- The Simulated TYD Word Processor --
type %1
```

Press the F6 key and the Enter key to complete the file. Now you are ready to use the simulated word processor. WP.BAT is a batch command file, and, by adding it to the disk, you have effectively added a command to DOS. That command is named WP. The %1 character in the TYPE command inside the WP.BAT file is what is known as a **command-line substitution**. When you execute the new WP command, DOS will substitute whatever you put on the command line for the %1. You will learn more about command-line substitutions in Chapter 9. Execute the WP command now, telling it to type the first letter to Aunt Milly.

```
A>wp \wordproc\docs\letters\milly01.ltr
```

This is an example of how you tell a command to access a file that is stored in a different subdirectory. The WP.BAT file will substitute the entire path and file name for its %1 parameter in its TYPE command, and you will see this display:

```
WP: ---- The Simulated TYD Word Processor ----
April 22, 1989

Dear Aunt Milly,
How are you? Wish you were here.
                    Sincerely yours,
                    Kilgore Trout

A>
```

COMMAND PATH PREFIXES

Sometimes when you are in a subdirectory, you will want to execute a command that is represented by a .COM, .EXE, or .BAT file in another subdirectory. One method for doing this is to use the DOS PATH command, and that technique is discussed in Chapter 5. But there is another way. When you issue the command, you can specify the subdirectory where the command file is stored. The subdirectory is prefixed to the command name just as a subdirectory can be prefixed to a file name.

Suppose you are logged onto the LETTERS subdirectory and want to use the new WP command that is in the SOFTWARE subdirectory in WP.BAT. To see how that works, first log onto the LETTERS subdirectory with this command:

```
A>cd \wordproc\docs\letters
```

If you were to try the WP command the same way you did in the previous exercise, DOS would display the following message:

```
Bad command or file name
```

This message means that DOS cannot find the WP.BAT file because you are logged onto the LETTERS subdirectory, and WP.BAT is in the SOFTWARE subdirectory. Instead, you can specify where the command is when you issue the command. Enter this version of the command:

```
A>\wordproc\software\wp milly01.ltr
```

This command works and gives the same display you saw earlier. Note that you did not need to specify the subdirectory where the MILLY01.LTR file is located. You are logged onto that subdirectory, so DOS has no trouble finding that file. If you were logged onto some other subdirectory where neither the software nor the document was located, you would need to specify paths for the WP.BAT software and the MILLY01.LTR data file. That command would look like this:

```
A>\wordproc\software\wp \wordproc\docs\letters\milly01.ltr
```

> The command just shown is verbose and would be difficult to remember. Because of its length, it is conducive to keying errors as well. You are well advised not to use this kind of command entry on a routine basis. How you set up your PC is up to you. Chapter 5 will ease this problem considerably. It describes the DOS PATH command, which lets DOS find software in other subdirectories without you specifying the pertinent subdirectory whenever you run the software.

FILE NAME SPECIFICATIONS

Now that you have used file names in a number of exercises, it is important to review the many ways you can specify a file on the DOS command line.

Disk File Names

The fully qualified, unambiguous DOS file name follows this format:

```
<drive>:<dos path>\<file name>.<extension>
```

The < drive > designator is the drive letter where the file is to be found. Drive letters are A, B, C, etc., through the highest drive letter installed on your computer. A colon must follow the drive letter if the letter is included. The drive letter is optional. If you leave it out, DOS and most applications programs assume that the file being specified is on the currently logged-on drive.

The < dos path > designator specifies the path through the subdirectories where the file is located. Each lower subdirectory name is prefixed with a backslash character to separate it from its parent. If the path does not begin with a backslash, DOS assumes that the first named subdirectory is subordinate to the currently logged-on directory. The path is optional. If you leave it out, DOS and most applications programs assume that the file being specified is in the currently logged-on subdirectory for the drive. If the path is given, there must be a backslash character to separate it from the file name.

The < file name > is from one to eight characters long and can consist of letters, numbers, and some special symbols. The file name can include the asterisk and/or the question mark wild cards.

Most file names include an extension as shown in the previous < extension > designator. The extension, which can be from one to three characters, is *not* mandatory. You can omit the extension when you create the file, in which case subsequent references to that file must be made without an extension. When an extension is used, it must be separated from the file name by a period. The extension can include the asterisk and/or the question mark wild cards.

Many applications programs allow you to specify file names from within the program rather than on the command line, and these programs usually use the same conventions for file names that DOS uses. Many applications programs will, however, append default extensions to files you name. You will need to be aware of any such extensions if you are going to use a DOS command to view or otherwise process the file from outside the application.

For example, your word processor software might allow you to identify your documents with the file name only, while the software appends something like .WP to the name. Later, when you want to delete, copy, or view a directory of those files, you'll need to know about the .WP extension you did not specify. The application's documentation should tell you if the program does that. When in doubt, use the DIR command after a session with the application to see what has been added or changed in your data file subdirectory.

Device Names

File names in a DOS command can be PC device (e.g., printer, modem, screen) specifiers. The effect is that the data content comes from or goes to the device rather than a file. You have already seen that you can copy the CON device to a file. You can specify the printer or a communications device (such as a modem) as well.

Following is a list of all device names:

CON	An input file is the keyboard; output is the screen.
PRN	The default printer, usually LPT1.
LPT1	The printer connected to physical printer port 1.
LPT2	The printer connected to physical printer port 2.
COM1	The device connected to communications port 1.
COM2	The device connected to communications port 2.
AUX	The default communications port, usually COM1.
NUL	The null device. There is no input. Output goes nowhere.

The NUL device is special. If you specify it where a command expects an output file, the output goes nowhere and is effectively lost. If you specify the NUL device where a command expects an input file, the command behaves as if the input file exists but is empty.

There are not many occasions where you will use device names instead of files, but consider this example. Enter the following command. (It is assumed that you have a printer connected and turned on.)

```
A>copy con prn
```

Type as many lines of text on the screen as you want. When you are done, press the F6 key and the Enter key. The text you typed is printed on the printer. You might use this technique to address an envelope, for example.

COPYING FILES (COPY)

You've been using the COPY command to build test files by copying from the console keyboard (CON) to the files named on the command line. But the COPY command has much more utility than that. It is the vehicle with which you copy files to diskettes to store them safely or to move them to another facility. COPY is the vehicle you use to import and install software from other sites. You will use the COPY command a lot (particularly for copying files from your hard disk to floppy disks for backup purposes). The format of the COPY command is shown here:

```
copy <source> <destination>
```

The <source> and <destination> designators are usually file name specifications with the optional drive, path, file names, wild cards, and extensions, as described earlier. They can also be device file names.

Copying Individual Files

Begin by logging onto the \WORDPROC\DOCS\LETTERS subdirectory where you have some text files to play with. Enter this command:

```
A>cd \wordproc\docs\letters
```

If you want, use the DIR command to see that the MILLY??.LTR files are still there.

Suppose you want to send the same letter to Uncle George that you sent to Aunt Milly. Rather than type the entire letter into a new file, you could make a copy of Milly's letter and use your word processor to change the salutation. This is a handy way to handle invitations, announcements, and other kinds of broadcast communications.

Make a copy of the MILLY01.LTR file, giving it another name. Enter this command:

```
A>copy milly01.ltr george.ltr
```

Use the DIR command to see that the copy has been made. You could now use your word processor to modify the letter for Uncle George.

Copying a File to Another Disk Drive

The COPY command has variations. For example, you can copy a file to another disk drive. Enter this command:

```
A>copy george.ltr c:
```

This command copies the GEORGE.LTR file from the A drive (where you are logged on) to the C drive as specified on the command line. Because you did not give a file name in the destination, the new file on the C drive will also be named GEORGE.LTR. The file is copied to whichever C drive subdirectory is currently logged on. Remember that you do not know how your PC is configured, so you do not know what subdirectory is logged on when you start these tutorial sessions.

Copying to a Specified Subdirectory

If you want to copy the file to a particular subdirectory on the C drive, you can name that subdirectory in the COPY command as shown in the following example. **Note:** Do not do this example as an exercise; it is merely an example. You do not know that the example subdirectory exists on your C drive, and you do not want to modify your hard disk's subdirectory structure in the name of these lessons.

```
A>copy george.ltr c:\wordproc\savearea
```

(This is an example—do not enter this command.)

Copying with Wild Cards

You can use wild cards in the file name. To copy all your letters to the C drive, enter this command:

```
A>copy *.* c:
```

Remember how wild cards work. The *.* specification calls out all file names and all extensions or, in other words, all files. This command says to copy all files in the current disk and subdirectory on the A drive to the C drive. You will see this display:

```
MILLY01.LTR
MILLY02.LTR
GEORGE.LTR
         3 File(s) copied
```

You do not want to leave those files on the C drive, so use the DEL command to delete them. Enter this command:

```
A>del c:*.ltr
```

Copying into the Current Subdirectory

So far, the COPY exercises have all had source (where files are being copied from) and destination, or target (where files are being copied to), specifiers. But if you leave out the destination, you tell DOS that the destination is the currently logged on disk and subdirectory and that the file names are to be the same as those in the source. For example, suppose you wanted to copy the letters from the LETTERS subdirectory to the MANUSCRP subdirectory. First, change to the MANUSCRP subdirectory with this command:

```
A>cd ..\manuscrp
```

Now copy the files by specifying the source parameter only. Because you are no longer logged onto the LETTERS subdirectory, you must specify the path to the files you want to copy. Enter this command:

```
A>copy ..\letters\*.*
```

To review, the dot-dot specifies the parent subdirectory on which you are logged. The LETTERS subdirectory is below the same parent, so its name appears next and is separated from the dot-dot parent with a backslash. The next backslash separates the path from the file name. The *.* is the wild card specification that specifies all files in the subdirectory. There is no destination file specification in the command. Therefore, this command says to copy all the files from the LETTERS subdirectory, which is on the same level under the same parent as the current subdirectory (MANUSCRP), and to copy those files into the current subdirectory.

In this kind of COPY where no destination is specified, the source file specification cannot point to the currently logged-on disk and path combination. Otherwise, you would be telling DOS to copy a file on top of itself, which DOS cannot do.

Copying Subdirectories

You can use the COPY command to copy entire subdirectories into the current one. You are currently logged onto \WORDPROC\DOCS\MANUSCRP.

Enter this command:

```
A>copy ..\letters
```

That file specification has no file name. It ends with the name of a subdirectory, the LETTERS subdirectory, so the specification tells the COPY command to copy all the files that are in the LETTERS subdirectory. You will see this display:

```
..\LETTERS\MILLY01.LTR
..\LETTERS\MILLY02.LTR
..\LETTERS\GEORGE.LTR
        3 File(s) copied
```

Once again, use the DIR command to see that all three letters have been copied into the MANUSCRP subdirectory. Then use the DEL command again to delete them.

Copying Several Files into One File

The COPY command can be used to copy several files into one file, linking together the source files so that the destination file is the combination of the source files. While still in the MANUSCRP subdirectory, enter this command:

```
A>copy milly01.ltr+milly02.ltr millies.ltr
```

You will see this display:

```
MILLY01.LTR
MILLY02.LTR
        1 File(s) copied
```

Note that although the COPY command has listed two files, it says at the bottom that only one file was copied. Use the DIR command to see that you built a new file named MILLIES.LTR. Its size is approximately the sum of the two files that were copied into it.

You can use wild cards to copy several files into one. Enter this command:

```
A>copy *.ltr letters.all
```

You will see this display:

```
MILLY01.LTR
MILLY02.LTR
GEORGE.LTR
MILLIES.LTR
        1 File(s)  copied
```

Once again, only one file was copied but, this time, four were listed. This count is an important clue. Suppose you wanted to copy all the files in the current subdirectory to a different subdirectory. But also suppose that you misspell the name of the destination subdirectory. Here is an example of such a mistake. Enter this command:

```
A>copy *.* \sprdsht\sheet
```

The mistake is in the spelling of the SHEETS subdirectory name. What you expect is to see a list of all the files, followed by a count of files copied. There are five files in the current subdirectory. But here is what would be displayed if you executed that erroneous command:

```
MILLY01.LTR
MILLY02.LTR
GEORGE.LTR
MILLIES.LTR
LETTERS.ALL
        1 File(s) copied
```

Because you misspelled SHEETS as SHEET, DOS thinks you mean to copy the files into one file named SHEET in the SPRDSHT subdirectory. Your clue that the COPY command did not work the way you expected it to is in the count of files copied. Because the count is one, you can tell that the files were copied to only one file instead of the five you expected. Run the DIR command against the SPRDSHT subdirectory now, and you will verify the error. Enter

```
A>dir \sprdsht
```

You will see this display:

```
Volume in drive A has no label
Directory of A:\SPRDSHT

.              <DIR>        4-22-89    8:50a
..             <DIR>        4-22-89    8:50a
SOFTWARE       <DIR>        4-24-89   10:30a
SHEETS         <DIR>        4-24-89   10:30a
SHEET             1180      4-25-89   12:07p
        5 File(s)    1123328 bytes free
```

Note that the size of the file might be different. The dates and times also will be different.

The SHEET file is a combination of the files you really wanted to copy into the SHEETS subdirectory. This circumstance results from the way the COPY command works. No doubt you will have this problem sometime, and no doubt you will not notice it. Copying will have become routine, and as long as you see no error message, you will seldom notice the little clue given by the file count. You can only hope that it does not cause too much inconvenience.

THE DEL COMMAND REVISITED

These last exercises have left some debris on the TYD Learning Diskette. You can use the DEL command to clear it up. The DEL command can be used to delete all the files in a subdirectory with this command:

```
A>del *.*
```

DOS recognizes that this command has serious implications. You have just said that you want to delete everything in the current subdirectory. DOS will ask the following question:

```
Are you sure (Y/N)?
```

Type the "Y," and DOS will delete the files.

If you use the DEL command on a subdirectory file, you are telling DOS to delete all the files in the subdirectory. The SPRDSHT subdirectory has one data file and two subdirectories. The DEL command does not extend below the specified subdirectory, so you can use the following command to delete the erroneous SHEET file from the SPRDSHT subdirectory:

```
A>del \sprdsht
```

The command just shown is the equivalent of this next command:

```
A>del \sprdsht\*.*
```

DOS will ask you to verify the delete by typing "Y" for yes.

RENAMING FILES

There will be times when you will want to rename a file. The DOS REN command is used to rename files. Its general format is as follows:

```
ren <oldname> <newname>
```

Change to the root directory for the next exercise. Enter this command:

```
A>cd \
```

Renaming Single Files

Suppose you want to make a new version of your AUTOEXEC.BAT file, but you do not want to lose the old one. You can rename the old file to something else and then create the new one. To rename AUTOEXEC.BAT to AUTOEXEC.SAV, enter this command:

```
A>ren autoexec.bat autoexec.sav
```

Now use the DIR command to see that the file still exists but with the new name.

If you do not change its name back or build a new AUTOEXEC.BAT, your next reload of DOS will be just like it was after you formatted the TYD Learning Diskette. Use this command to reset the name.

```
A>ren autoexec.sav autoexec.bat
```

Renaming Groups of Files

You can rename groups of files with one command by using wild cards. Change to the LETTERS subdirectory with this command:

```
A>cd \wordproc\docs\letters
```

Rename all the letter files so that the extension changes from .LTR to .TXT. Enter this command:

```
A>ren *.ltr *.txt
```

Use the DIR command to see that the file name extensions have changed.

Renaming Files in Other Places

You can rename files on other disk drives or in other subdirectories by specifying the drive and path in the first (old name) parameter. The second (new name) parameter does not need to be qualified with a path specification.

You are currently logged onto the \WORDPROC\DOCS\LETTERS subdirectory. To change the name of the WP.BAT file, which is in the \WORDPROC\SOFTWARE subdirectory, to EDIT.BAT, enter

```
A>ren \wordproc\software\wp.bat edit.bat
```

Use the DIR command to see that the WP.BAT file is now named EDIT.BAT.

Putting Everything Back

Now perform some housekeeping. First, use REN to give the word processor batch file its original name. Enter this command:

```
A>ren \wordproc\software\edit.bat wp.bat
```

Next, delete the GEORGE.TXT file from the LETTERS subdirectory with this command:

```
A>del george.txt
```

Finally, rename the letter files so they have the .LTR extensions again. Enter

```
A>ren *.txt *.ltr
```

BUILDING THE DOS SUBDIRECTORY

For the series of exercises in the chapters that follow, you will need to add a number of the DOS utility programs to the TYD Learning Diskette. You cannot know where those programs are on your system. Many installers place them on the C drive in a subdirectory named DOS, and it is assumed that your system was installed that way.

If the following procedure gives you trouble, use the CD and DIR commands to poke around in your hard disk until you find the files in question. You must copy the files you need to the TYD Learning Diskette with the following commands. (**Hint**: use the F1 and F3 keys to copy duplicated keystrokes in a command that is similar to the one entered just before it.)

```
A>cd \dos
A>copy c:\dos\backup.com
A>copy c:\dos\chkdsk.com
A>copy c:\dos\diskcopy.com
A>copy c:\dos\edlin.com
A>copy c:\dos\format.com
A>copy c:\dos\label.com
A>copy c:\dos\mode.com
A>copy c:\dos\more.com
A>copy c:\dos\restore.com
A>copy c:\dos\tree.com
A>copy c:\dos\find.exe
A>copy c:\dos\sort.exe
A>copy c:\dos\xcopy.exe
A>copy c:\dos\ansi.sys
```

SUMMARY

You have taken in a lot of knowledge in this chapter. These exercises have prepared you to use as much of DOS's power as most users will ever need. Certainly you are now ready to use the PC in the manner prescribed by whomever installed the system. If nothing else has been accomplished, you can now find your data files and copy them to a safe place for backup purposes.

The next chapter explains the DOS PATH command and its implications. You often need to set the DOS PATH when you install new applications software, and Chapter 5 explains what the PATH is, what it does, and how you set it.

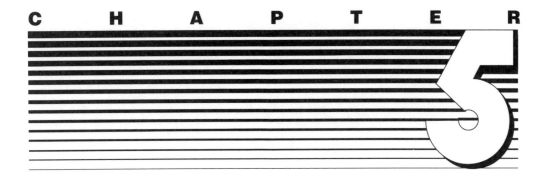

THE DOS PATH

If you organize your data files in one subdirectory and your software in another as you did on the TYD Learning Diskette, you must specify where one or the other is located. Because you can be logged onto only one place at a time, if you are logged onto where the software is located, you must tell the programs where to find the data files, and if you are logged onto where the data files are located, you must tell DOS where to find the software.

This chapter describes the DOS PATH variable, a mechanism that allows DOS to find command files that are in remote drives and subdirectories.

What you will learn in this chapter:

- The PATH variable
- The PATH command

SIMULATING A SPREADSHEET

In Chapter 4, you built a simulated word processor called WP.BAT. You will use that software in this chapter, too, but you need another software file to show the versatility of the PATH, so you will simulate a spreadsheet program as well.

Use the COPY command as before to build the spreadsheet data and command files. Build the command file by entering this command:

```
A>copy con \sprdsht\software\ss.bat
```

Now, enter these lines of text (remember to press Enter at the end of each line):

```
echo off
cls
echo SS: ---- The Simulated TYD Spreadsheet ----

type %1
```

Press the F6 key followed by the Enter key. This batch command file will display the file you name on the command line. It is functionally equivalent to the WP.BAT file except that it has its own program title so you can tell them apart.

Next, build a simulated spreadsheet data file with this command:

```
A>copy con \sprdsht\sheets\taxes88.sps
```

Type some lines of spreadsheet data like this:

```
Gross Income:      25000.00
Bracket:                .10
Taxes:              2500.00
```

Press the F6 key and then the Enter key.

Finally, so you also have a file in your word processor, build a manuscript file called NOVEL.DOC for the WP simulated word processor by entering this command:

```
A>copy con \wordproc\docs\manuscrp\novel.doc
```

Type some deathless prose, such as the following:

```
Illusions on the Moors - Chapter 1.

It was a cold and stormy night.
Tiffany pulled her lace shawl about her
bare shoulders and shuddered in the cold air.
The count smiled at her and beckoned for
her to follow him down the corridor and
into the bedchambers.
```

Press the F6 key and then the Enter key. That file concludes the test data.

Figure 5.1 shows the full contents of the TYD Learning Diskette with these new files added.

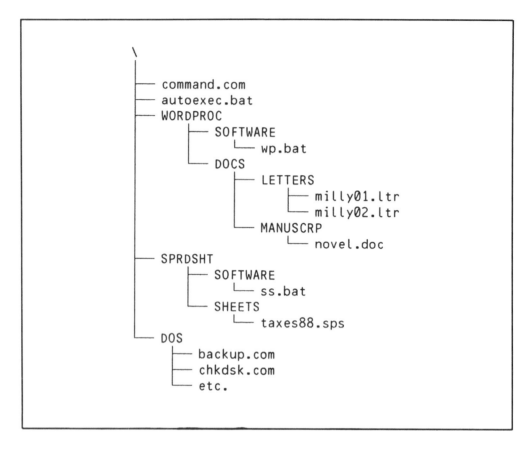

Figure 5.1   The TYD Learning Diskette

HOW DOS FINDS THE COMMANDS

When you organize a subdirectory hierarchy, you nearly always have one copy of each software package and then several categories of data files that the software package processes. That is the situation simulated on the TYD Learning Diskette. You have one word processor and two different kinds of documents — letters and manuscripts.

The usual way to access your data files with your software programs is to log onto the subdirectory in which the data files are kept and run the software from the subdirectory in which you keep the program. Up until now, you have done that, but you have always specified the path to the program when you issued its command. In Chapter 4, you ran the word processor while logged onto the LETTERS subdirectory by entering this command:

```
A>\wordproc\software\wp milly01.ltr
```

This command will always work, of course, but it has disadvantages. You are required to remember where everything is stored, and you must type the path whenever you want to use a command.

The PATH Variable

DOS has a mechanism called the DOS PATH variable that provides a shortcut to locating your software. The PATH specifies a subdirectory path that DOS will search when it is looking for a .BAT, .COM, or .EXE file that you have issued as a command. The PATH consists of one or more drives and subdirectory paths. The PATH is called a variable because you can change its value with the DOS PATH command.

If a PATH has been specified, DOS looks first in the currently logged-on drive and subdirectory, and, if the command file is not there, DOS searches the specified path for it. If no PATH has been specified, DOS looks for the command file only in the currently logged-on drive and subdirectory. Up until now, no PATH has been specified in the exercises.

The PATH Command

You set the PATH variable with the PATH command. You can also view the current path by issuing the PATH command with no parameters. Enter this command:

```
A>path
```

You will see this display:

```
No Path
```

That message means that no PATH has been established. Review what happens when you try to run software that DOS cannot find. First, log onto the MANUSCRP subdirectory where you put that great novel. Enter this command:

```
A>cd \wordproc\docs\manuscrp
```

Figure 5.2 shows where you are logged on and that DOS can find no software. There are no command files in the MANUSCRP subdirectory, and DOS has no PATH to search.

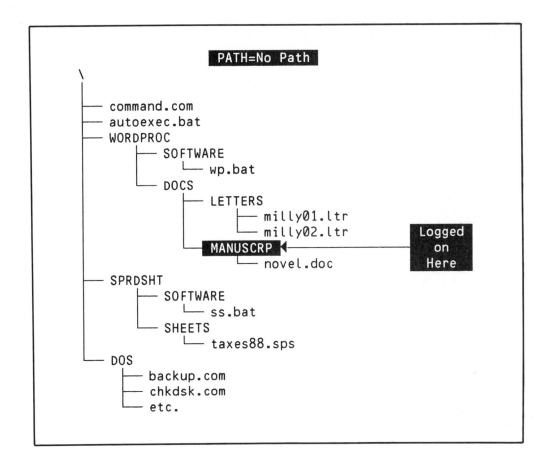

Figure 5.2   No path, no software

To illustrate this point, try to use the WP command to display the novel without specifying the software's path:

```
A>wp novel.doc
```

DOS responds with this error message:

```
Bad command or file name
```

This message means that DOS cannot find the WP.BAT file because you are logged onto the MANUSCRP subdirectory, and WP.BAT is in the SOFTWARE subdirectory.

Setting the PATH

Earlier you had to specify where the command was stored when you issued it on the command line. But now you know that if you can specify the path to the software in the DOS PATH variable, DOS will be able to find the software. Do so with this command:

```
A>path=a:\wordproc\software
```

Viewing the PATH

Now use the PATH command with no parameters to see that the PATH variable has been set. Enter this command:

```
A>path
```

You will see this display:

```
PATH=A:\WORDPROC\SOFTWARE
```

Figure 5.3 shows that even though you are logged onto the MANUSCRP subdirectory, DOS can find the command file that is stored in SOFTWARE.

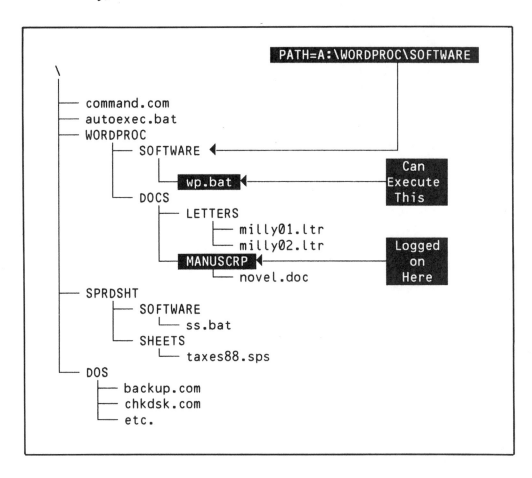

Figure 5.3   A path to WP.BAT

Using the PATH

Try again to use the WP command to display the novel without specifying the software's path:

```
A>wp novel.doc
```

The command works because DOS found the WP.BAT file by searching the PATH you established. You will see this display:

```
WP: ---- The Simulated TYD Word Processor ----
Illusions on the Moors - Chapter 1.

It was a cold and stormy night.
Tiffany pulled her lace shawl about her
bare shoulders and shuddered in the cold air.
The count smiled at her and beckoned for
her to follow him down the corridor and
into the bedchambers.
```

Multiple Paths

As you saw in Figure 5.3, the PATH you've used so far leads to one subdirectory only. If word processing was all you ever needed to do, that would be enough. But most users use the PC for several tasks, and every user needs to use the DOS utility programs once in a while. A single path is not enough.

The TYD Learning Diskette includes the SS.BAT simulated spreadsheet in the SPRDSHT subdirectory, and it is presumed that you would want to run spreadsheets too (for example, a typical spreadsheet program is Lotus 1-2-3). You could issue the PATH command every time you wanted to change from word processing to spreadsheet processing, but that would be less efficient than simply typing the path on the command line when you issue the commands that run your programs. You are looking for a better way, not a less efficient way.

As you might expect, the PATH command allows you to identify several paths for DOS to search. To see how that works, enter the following command:

```
A>path=a:\wordproc\software;a:\sprdsht\software
```

Note that there are two distinct paths in this command, and they are separated by a semicolon. When you issue a command, DOS will search using this sequence. First, the currently logged-on subdirectory is searched. If the command file is not found, the \WORDPROC\SOFTWARE subdirectory is searched. If the command file is still not found, the \SPRDSHT\SOFTWARE subdirectory is searched.

Figure 5.4 shows the effect of the command just issued. You can now execute WP.BAT and SS.BAT regardless of where you are logged on.

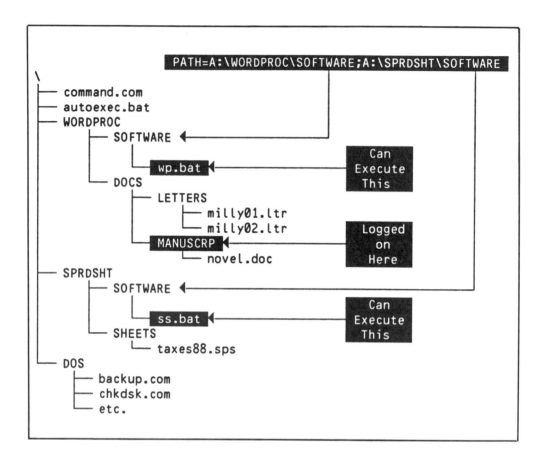

Figure 5.4   Multiple paths

Running the Spreadsheet

Issue this command to change to the **SHEETS** subdirectory:

```
A>cd \SPRDSHT\SHEETS
```

Now run the SS.BAT command against the TAXES88.SPS file with this command:

```
A>ss taxes88.sps
```

You have successfully run the simulated spreadsheet, and you will see this display:

```
SS: ---- The Simulated TYD Spreadsheet ----
Gross Income:    25000.00
Bracket:              .10
Taxes:            2500.00
```

A PATH to DOS

No matter what your applications, whether they be word processing, spreadsheets, desktop publishing, data bases, CAD/CAM, software development, or custom applications, you will frequently use the DOS utility programs. In anticipation of the advanced exercises in Chapter 7, you have already copied some of these programs into the DOS subdirectory on the TYD Learning Diskette. You will want a PATH to these programs as well. Enter this command:

```
A>path=a:\wordproc\software;a:\sprdsht\software;a:\dos
```

This command adds the DOS subdirectory to the DOS PATH. Figure 5.5 shows the effect of this path.

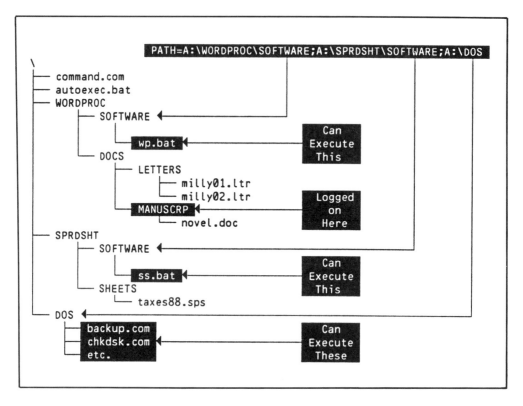

Figure 5.5   Paths to DOS utility programs

The PATH Command in AUTOEXEC.BAT

You do not want to type a long PATH command in every time you load DOS. Why not add the command to your AUTOEXEC.BAT file? Then it will be automatically executed whenever you reload DOS, and your path will be established. You can just forget about setting the path, then. Enter this command:

```
A>copy con autoexec.bat
```

Then type these lines:

```
echo off
cls
echo Teach Yourself DOS Learning Diskette
ver
path=a:\wordproc\software;a:\sprdsht\software;a:\dos
```

Press F6 and then the Enter key, and your new AUTOEXEC.BAT file will be built.

Press Ctrl-Alt-Del to reboot your PC. Then enter this command to see that your path has automatically been set:

```
A>path
```

You will see this display:

```
Path=A:\WORDPROC\SOFTWARE;A:\SPRDSHT\SOFTWARE;A:\DOS
```

Commands with the Same Name

You might have guessed that it is possible to have command files with the same name in different subdirectories. For example, you could build another subdirectory and put a file named WP.BAT in it. This subdirectory construction is perfectly legitimate in DOS. If you logged onto that new subdirectory and issued the WP command, the new WP.BAT command would be executed because DOS looks in the currently logged-on subdirectory first for command files. If you logged onto a different subdirectory and issued the command, the old WP.BAT command would be executed because that is the one DOS would find as it searched the paths.

Suppose two subdirectories that both contained WP.BAT files were in the DOS PATH. Then DOS would execute the first one it found. DOS searches the paths in the sequence in which they are specified in the PATH command, beginning with the left-most path.

It is not a good idea to have different programs on your system with the same name, but sometimes that situation is hard to avoid. For example, many applications software systems include command files named INSTALL and README. When you run into these conflicts, it is best to keep a keen eye on what you are doing and make sure you are running the correct command file.

Invalid Subdirectories in the PATH

DOS does not complain if you specify a path that does not exist. DOS sets it up and registers its objection the first time it needs to use that path. Enter this command:

```
A>path=\nonsense
```

Now issue the PATH command:

```
A>path
```

DOS thinks there is a path to a subdirectory called NONSENSE. You will see this display:

```
PATH=NONSENSE
```

DOS has not complained yet. Now try to execute the WP command.

```
A>wp
```

DOS cannot find WP.BAT, and says so with this error message, which looks just like the one you received when there was no path:

```
Bad command or file name
```

Invalid Drives in the PATH

DOS will let you know if the path contains an invalid disk drive. Enter this command:

```
A>path=g:\nonsense
```

The assumption here is that your PC has no G drive. (Most do not, but some networked PCs will have drives well up into the alphabet.) Now try the WP command again:

```
A>wp
```

Now you not only receive the earlier error message, you also receive a clue as to what is wrong:

```
Invalid drive in search path
Bad command or file name
```

SUMMARY

With this chapter under your belt, you are ready to use your PC and look almost like a master. You are not a full-fledged Power User yet, but most folks will not be able to tell because your knowledge at this point will serve you well for most of your PC usage.

The next chapter explains a class of commands called "filters," a DOS curiosity called a "pipe," and how you can use the unique properties of the DOS command line to tie such features together for some interesting effects.

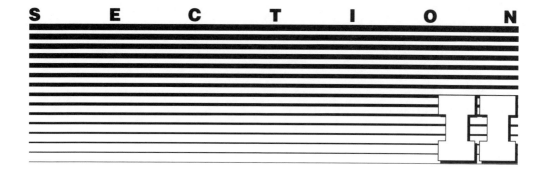

THE POWER USER

You have come a long way. You are now equipped to use DOS in ways that will support most of your work. But DOS has many fascinating and useful extensions. These are features that you could ignore and maybe never miss. If you have enough under your belt to get the job done, you can quit learning now. But you are encouraged to look through these next few chapters to get a glimpse at some of the potential that DOS offers you, for these are the basic tools of the Power User.

If you do stop now, return here in a few weeks or months after you have more experience with DOS. By then you will have better insight into the kinds of operations you wish you could perform. Perhaps some of these operations are covered in this section.

This section is not a comprehensive treatment of Power User tools and techniques. Its purpose, now that you have learned the basic principles of DOS operation, is to stir your imagination and introduce you to some of the advanced DOS features. If it arouses your curiosity and gets you thinking, you will invent more uses for these tools than any book could possibly cover.

131

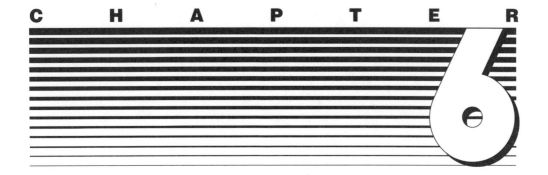

C H A P T E R

6

FILTERS, PIPES, AND INPUT/OUTPUT REDIRECTION

This chapter is about a special kind of DOS command called the "filter" command and about the DOS pipes and I/O redirection that support filters. Not all commands are filters, but the ones that are can be executed in unique ways to achieve some interesting results. You do not know it, but you already used several DOS filters in Section I.

You could live happily all your life without using the features of a filter, but it is helpful to know what filters are and how they work. Many DOS commands are filters, but you do not always need to know that to use them. Most of your applications programs are not filters. To use the full power of filter commands, you must understand them, and this chapter explains them.

What you will learn in this chapter:

- What a filter is
- How to redirect a filter's input and output

- How to connect filters with a pipe
- Some practical applications for filters

As with the rest of *Teach Yourself DOS*, this chapter does not tell the whole story because you do not need the whole story to gain the benefits from these commands and features. Later, when you become a seasoned DOS user, you might want to dig into your DOS documentation and the more advanced DOS books to gain a deeper understanding of pipes, filters, and input/output redirection.

THE FILTER

DOS supports a category of commands called a **filter**. A filter is a program that reads and writes text. More specifically, it reads text from what is called the **standard input device** and writes text to the **standard output device**. Some filters have no input. Unless you redirect (or redesignate) the input and output devices, input comes from the keyboard and output goes to the screen.

Not all applications commands are filters, but many DOS commands are. Word processors, spreadsheets, data base programs, and other custom applications are not usually written to be filters even though they read from the keyboard and write to the screen. These programs have broader concerns than the translation of an input text stream to an output text stream, and their developers chose not to implement them as filters.

Figure 6.1 is a diagram of a filter program that has no input. You have already run several such filters in the exercises in preceding chapters. The DOS DIR and TYPE commands are examples of filters that have no input except what is specified on the command line. When you issue the DIR command, DOS writes the directory display to the standard output device (in this case, the screen). When you issue the TYPE command, DOS writes the file display to the standard output device.

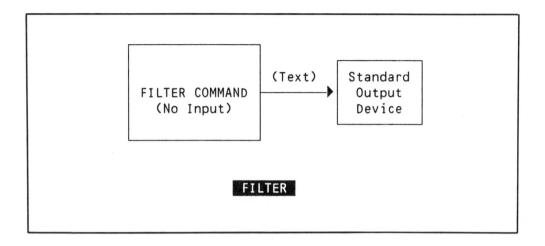

Figure 6.1   Simple FILTER command

Figure 6.2 is a diagram of a filter program that has both input and output. The DATE and TIME commands are examples of filters with input and output. When you execute either command with no command-line parameters, the date and time are written to the standard output device along with the prompts to enter a new date and time. The new date and time (or the pressing of the Enter key when no date and time are specified) are read from the standard input device.

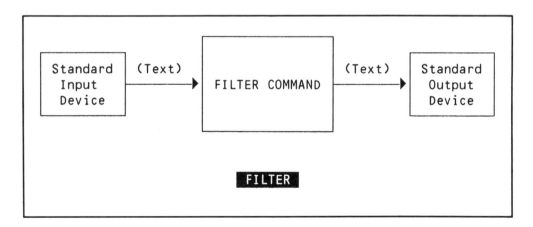

Figure 6.2   FILTER with input/ouput

So far in this book the standard input device has always been the keyboard, and the standard output device has always been the screen. Later you will see how the input to filters can come from other places and how the output to filters can be used in other ways.

The filter command category is well named. A filter reads lines of text and filters them into modified lines of text. Filters that have no standard input get the data to modify from other places.

STANDARD INPUT AND OUTPUT DEVICES

Filter programs read and write text. The text they read comes from the generic device that DOS calls the "standard input device." The text they write goes to the generic "standard output device." These devices are always the keyboard and the screen, respectively, unless you tell DOS otherwise.

When you run a filter program, you can specify that its text input *comes* from anywhere – another physical input device, a disk file, or another program. When you do this, the standard input device becomes what you have told DOS it will be.

When you run a filter program, you can specify that its text output *goes* to anywhere – another physical output device, a disk file, or another program. When you do this, the standard output device becomes what you have told DOS it will be.

INPUT/OUTPUT REDIRECTION

The power of using standard devices becomes apparent when you consider the ability to redirect the data. Any program that takes text input from the standard input device can get that text from any file or input device. The program does not know or care where the text comes from; it simply reads whatever text DOS provides on the standard input device. Any program that writes text to the standard output device can write that text to a file or device.

When you run a filter from the command line, you can tell DOS that the input is to come from somewhere other than the keyboard. For example, you can tell DOS that the input is to be found in a disk file. Figure 6.3 shows input redirection. The filter command reads its text from the standard input device, but DOS has substituted the contents of the disk input file for what you would normally type on the keyboard.

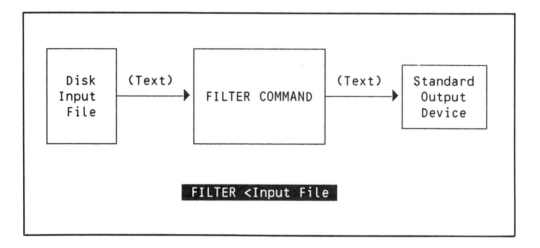

Figure 6.3   Redirected input

To redirect input from a file, you include the less-than (<) character on the command line, followed by the name of the file.

You can also tell DOS that the output is to be written to a disk file. Figure 6.4 shows this relationship. The filter command writes its text to the standard output device, but DOS has substituted the disk output file to receive what you would normally see on the screen.

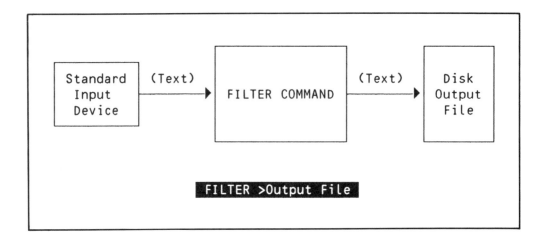

Figure 6.4   Redirected output

To redirect output to a file, you include the greater-than (>) character on the command line, followed by the name of the file to be created. If you name a file that already exists, DOS replaces that file with the new one.

THE SORT FILTER

DOS has a utility filter program called SORT. This program reads lines of text from the standard input device, sorts those lines of text into alphabetical sequence, and writes the sorted output text to the standard output device. First, see how SORT behaves when there is no input/output redirection. Enter this command:

```
A>sort
```

The cursor will wait at the left margin of the screen for you to type. Enter some lines of text that you want to have sorted:

```
There
was
a
young
man
from
Nantucket
```

Press the F6 key and then the Enter key. The SORT filter will sort your lines of text alphabetically and display the sorted text on the screen:

```
a
from
man
Nantucket
there
was
young
```

This exercise demonstrates the function of a filter, but not its usefulness. To derive any benefit from the SORT filter, you would want to sort files. The silly limerick just used would have little meaning in its sorted version. But there are occasions when you will want to sort some real data files.

To illustrate this point, build a file of names and birthdays. You will build it in no sequence at all to begin. Use the COPY command to build the file:

```
A>copy con names.dat
```

Type some data records in a fixed format of columns as shown here:

```
Marvel, Captain    1950/01/01
Washington, Geo.   1732/02/22
Brown, Clifford    1956/06/26
Tatum, Art         1910/10/13
```

Press the F6 key followed by the Enter key to store the file. Now you are ready to sort it. To test your sort, try it without redirecting the output. If what has been discussed works, the file should be sorted and sent to the screen. Enter this command:

```
A>sort <names.dat
```

You will see the sorted data displayed on the screen like this:

```
Brown, Clifford    1956/06/26
Marvel, Captain    1950/01/01
Tatum, Art         1910/10/13
Washington, Geo.   1732/02/22
```

Sorting files to the screen has some use, but you will more often want to sort a file and write the sorted data to another file for processing by another program. Figure 6.5 shows how a filter can read from one file and write to another.

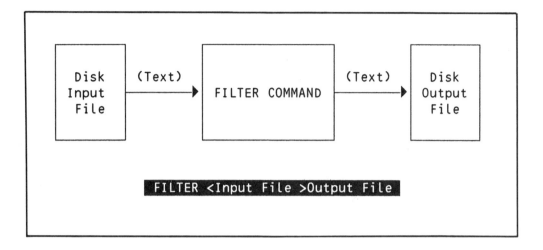

Figure 6.5   Redirected input and output

To sort the NAMES.DAT file and retain the results, enter this command:

```
A>sort <names.dat >names.srt
```

This command tells the SORT filter to read the file named NAMES.DAT, sort it, and write the sorted information to a file named NAMES.SRT. There is no screen display associated with this command. Use the DIR command to see that the NAMES.SRT file was created. Use the TYPE command to view the file.

The SORT command collates the text, starting in the first column (e.g., the "W" in "Washington"). But you can tell it to start in a different column. The NAMES.DAT file includes dates that are in year/month/day sequence and that start in column 18 (the "1" in "1732"). You can sort on these dates with this command:

```
A>sort <names.dat /+18
```

The output will be in this sequence:

```
Washington, Geo.    1732/02/22
Tatum, Art          1910/10/13
Marvel, Captain     1950/01/01
Brown, Clifford     1956/06/26
```

DIR AND TYPE AS FILTERS

The DIR and TYPE commands are each one half of a filter in that their displays are written to the standard output device. For example, enter this command:

```
A>dir >latest.dir
```

This command will write the directory on drive A> to the file named LATEST.DIR. This feature is useful in preparing operating procedures for your system. It has even more utility when used with the DOS pipe described later in this chapter.

The TYPE command will send its output to a file the same way. Try this command:

```
A>type latest.dir >typed.dir
```

This command types the LATEST.DIR file, sending the typed result to a new file named TYPED.DIR. It has the same effect as copying one file to the other with the COPY command.

A lot of this will make more sense by the time you finish this chapter.

THE FIND FILTER

The FIND filter reads lines of text from the standard input device and writes selected lines of that text to the standard output device. The selection is a function of the parameters you include on the command line. Suppose you wanted to see all the records in the NAMES.DAT file that had dates in the fifties. The FIND filter can find them for you. Enter this command:

```
A>find "195" <names.dat
```

This command says to read the file named NAMES.DAT and write out every line that contains the value, "195." This was the criterion chosen for the selection of dates in the fifties. You would see this display:

```
Marvel, Captain  1950/01/01
Brown, Clifford  1956/06/26
```

Of course, if you wanted this subset of the original file to be written to another disk file, you would use output redirection on the command line, as shown here:

```
A>find "195" <names.dat >names.195
```

This command will write the selected records to a new file named NAMES.195.

A variation of the FIND command allows you to select all the records that do not match the criterion. That variation is invoked by the /V command-line option, as shown here:

```
A>find /V "195" <names.dat
```

This command would provide this display, which could have been sent to a file instead:

```
Washington, Geo.  1732/02/22
Tatum, Art        1910/10/13
```

There are two other command-line options. The first is the /C option, which displays a count of the number of lines that match the criterion. Enter this command:

```
A>find /C "195" <names.dat
```

The FIND program will return the number 2 on the screen because it finds two lines of text that match the criterion.

The other option is the /N option, which displays the line number in the file where the matches occur. Enter this command:

```
A>find /N "195" <names.dat
```

You will see this display:

```
[1]Marvel, Captain  1950/01/01
[3]Brown, Clifford  1956/06/26
```

This feature is useful if you will then be using a text editor to work on the text file. Knowing the line numbers of the matching text lines will help you find them.

THE MORE FILTER

The MORE filter is particularly handy when you are dealing with large text files that you want to display. You have no large text file on the TYD Learning Diskette, but perhaps you know of one on another disk. For this example, assume that it is named LONG.DOC and that it is on the C drive. Suppose you entered this command:

```
more <c:long.doc
```

The MORE filter would read the standard input and write one screenful of information to the standard output device. Then it would display the message "--More--" at the bottom of the screen and wait for a keystroke. The keystroke would be taken from the keyboard regardless of whether the standard input device was redirected (which it usually is).

This filter allows you to view long text files without worrying about them scrolling off the screen faster than you can read them.

APPENDING TEXT TO A FILE

Output redirection normally creates a new file, replacing any existing file with the same name. A variation on output redirection allows you to append (or concatenate) to an existing file what is written to the standard output device. To append to a file, you use the concatenation (> >) symbol rather than the redirection (>) symbol on the command line. Figure 6.6 depicts this operation:

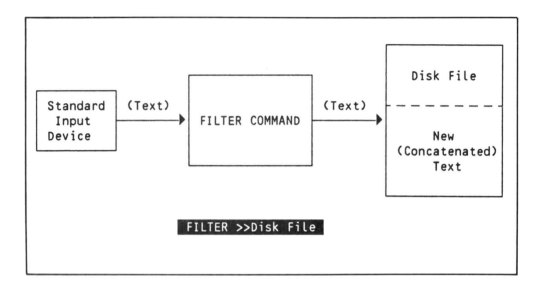

Figure 6.6   Concatenating text

For example, to add some lines to the NAMES.DAT file, enter these commands:

```
A>echo Armstrong, Louis 1900/07/04 >>names.dat
A>echo Stauffer, Judy   1941/11/17 >>names.dat
```

The ECHO command is a filter; its output is sent to the standard output device. In this case, ECHO was used to append text to the NAMES.DAT file. Each execution of the command performs an additional append.

REDIRECTING OUTPUT TO A PRINTER

The standard output device can be redirected to a DOS device. The most common use of this feature is to print something. To redirect the standard output device to the printer, you use the PRN device name instead of a file name after the output redirection (>) symbol. Figure 6.7 shows this operation.

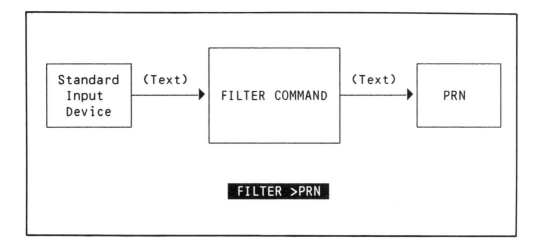

Figure 6.7   Redirecting output to the printer

Perhaps, for example, you want a hard copy of the directory of a diskette in the A drive. Make sure your printer is connected and turned on, and enter this command:

```
A>dir >prn
```

The directory will be printed. You can also redirect output to the LPT1, LPT2, LPT3, COM1, and COM2 devices. These devices are usually printers or modems connected to your computer.

REDIRECTING OUTPUT TO A NUL DEVICE

When you redirect output to the NUL device, you effectively disable the output. This is most often used in batch files (described in Chapter 9) when you do not want to see a particular message. For example, if you routinely copy a file or files, perhaps as a procedure to back up (save for later use) your data files, you might have the COPY commands in a batch file. Normally, the COPY command displays the number of files copied. At other times, all the files are not there to be copied, and the COPY command issues a "File not found" message. You might not want to see those messages.

Try this command to see the effect of an erroneous COPY command:

```
A>copy xxx yyy
```

You will see this display:

```
XXX File not found
        0 File(s) copied
```

To suppress the output displayed by the COPY command, use this version of it:

```
A>copy xxx yyy >nul
```

PIPES

The real power of input/output redirection is realized when you use DOS pipes. A **pipe** is a DOS mechanism that connects two filter programs. The standard output of the first filter becomes the standard input of the second filter. Both programs are named on the command line and are connected by the pipe (|) symbol, which will appear as a split line on your screen (see Figure 6.8).

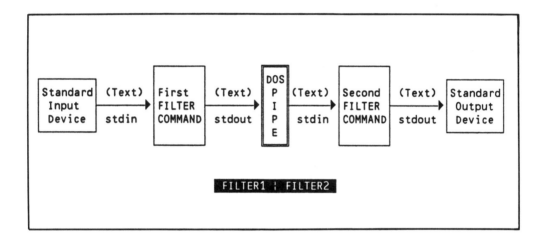

Figure 6.8   The DOS pipe

Several filters can be strung together with pipes on the command line. For example, suppose you wanted a directory of all files that were not subdirectories and you wanted them sorted by file name. Furthermore, because you expect a lot of files in the display, you want the display to pause at each screenful of file names. You could use this command:

```
A>dir | find /V "<DIR>" | sort | more
```

This command sequence executes the DIR command first. Because the DIR command is followed by the pipe (|) symbol, the entire directory is written to the DOS pipe. Then the FIND filter is executed, and because the command name follows a pipe symbol, FIND reads its input from the DOS pipe. The next entry on the command line is the /V option, which tells FIND to select all lines from the pipe that do not match the " < DIR >" value. This will eliminate the subdirectories from the directory listing. This subset of the directory from FIND is piped into the SORT filter, which sorts the directory and sends the sorted directory through the DOS pipe to the MORE filter. The MORE filter reads the sorted directory from the pipe and sends it one page at a time to the standard output device, which is, finally, the screen.

> Take a moment to consider what you've learned. Imagine how the command you just executed would have looked before you began this book. Gobbledygook. You can see why beginning DOS users are intimidated by the complexity of the DOS command line. You can also see why well-meaning system designers and installers try to shield users from this cryptic command language with shells and menu programs. Yet, now that you understand as much as you do, you can begin to appreciate the concise elegance of command-line control.

SOME PRACTICAL APPLICATIONS

Pipes, filters, and input/output redirection offer more than just a study in elegance. There are practical applications for filters that you can begin to use right away.

Remember that filters work with files of text. You will not run your spreadsheets, data bases, or word processing documents through a filter. Certainly, all these files look like text as they are presented to you by their applications programs, but most such data files contain embedded, non-text control data that would confuse most filters.

The best test to see if a data file is acceptable to a filter is to use the TYPE command to display it on the screen. If the information displays cleanly, chances are other filters will be able to process it. If, however, you see a lot of strange characters and hear an occasional beep, forget using the file with filters. It contains non-textual data.

Chaining FIND Commands

Earlier, you used the FIND command to filter unwanted lines of text from a directory and to select specific lines from a data file, but suppose you wanted the select criteria to be a complex set of selectors. Consider NAMES.DAT, shown here again:

```
Marvel, Captain     1950/01/01
Washington, Geo.    1732/02/22
Brown, Clifford     1956/06/26
Tatum, Art          1910/10/13
```

Suppose you wanted to select those records with dates in the 1900s but nothing from the month of June. You could enter this command:

```
A>find " 19" <names.dat | find /V "/06/"
```

This command tells the FIND filter to select all records from NAMES.DAT that have the value " 19." (The leading space before "19" prevents the selection of records that might have "19" as the day. None do in this case, but you won't always know that when you run the command.) The filtered records are then piped through a second execution of FIND, which filters out all records with the value "/06/." The result is this display:

```
Marvel, Captain     1950/01/01
Tatum, Art          1910/10/13
```

Filtering Directly to the Printer

Remember that the standard output device can be a device other than the screen. It can be the printer. If you redirect the output from a filter to the PRN device, the text output will be displayed rather than printed. Turn your printer on and try this command:

```
A>dir > prn
```

The directory goes to the printer rather than to the screen.

Suppose you routinely print your return addresses onto envelopes and you do not want to load your behemoth word processor every time to do it. You can build this batch file, which you might name DINOS.BAT:

```
echo Dino's Jazz Lounge >prn
echo 315 W. Cocoa Beach Causeway >prn
echo Cocoa Beach, FL 32931 >prn
```

Insert an envelope in the printer and enter the DINOS command. For each additional envelope, press F3 to save keystrokes. You are on your way to becoming a Power User. Chapter 9 contains more details on batch files.

Many printers are programmable. You send them what are called **setup strings** to set their character size, pitch, underlining, boldface, fonts, and many other controls. Most users do not concern themselves with these matters, allowing their applications programs to control printing. It is possible however to use the ECHO filter to send simple command strings to the printer. This method is for those times when you want to print something a certain way and your word processor and spreadsheet programs are not involved.

First, you must know the command strings that your printer uses. Many of these are what are called "Escape sequences," strings that begin with the ESC character (ESC stands for "Escape" and is one of the set of characters called the ASCII character set). For example, the EPSON FX80 series of printers uses the following sequence of characters to turn on boldface printing:

```
<esc>E
```

The <esc> token represents the ASCII Escape character. You cannot enter this character into a file with the COPY CON <filename> method used so far in this book. You must use a text editor program, and that program must allow the entry of the Escape character. You must use an editor that does allow entry of the Escape character. The EDLIN text editor included with DOS and described in Chapter 8 does allow it. See Chapter 8 for a description of this technique.

With many full-screen text editor programs, to enter the Escape character into a text file, you hold down the Alt and Shift keys with the NumLock toggle off (a toggle key is one that goes into effect when you press the key and ceases being in effect when you press the key a second time) and press the 2 key followed by the 7 key on the numeric keypad. If a small arrow pointing to the left appears, the Escape key is inserted into the text.

To change an EPSON FX80 printer to boldface, put the following command into a batch file named BOLD.BAT. You must use a cooperating text editor program such as EDLIN to build this file. The arrow is the Escape character.

```
echo ←E >prn
```

Once you have built the BOLD.BAT file, enter the BOLD command to put your printer into boldface mode. (See Chapter 8 for an exercise that builds BOLD.BAT with EDLIN.)

Finding a File on the Disk

One of the most frequent complaints of new users is that they cannot find a file on a disk after they have created it. Applications software and system installers have a diabolical way of hiding files in the depths of the subdirectory structure.

You might some day wonder if a given file is on the disk and, if so, where it is. DOS has a filter command named TREE, which displays the subdirectory structure of a disk. This filter can also be used to display the files in the subdirectories. To see the entire structure of the TYD Learning Diskette, enter this command:

```
A>tree /f | more
```

The typical TREE display is lengthy. You should use the MORE command as shown here or redirect the display to a file. Here is the TREE display, which you would see one screenful at a time with the command just entered. (Note that the /f option allows you to see the names of the files in each subdirectory. Without the /f option, only the subdirectories will be listed.)

```
DIRECTORY PATH LISTING
Files:              COMMAND .COM
                   AUTOEXEC.BAT
                   NAMES   .DAT
                   NAMES   .SRT

Path: \WORDPROC
```

```
Sub-directories:   SOFTWARE
                   DOCS

Files:             None

Path: \WORDPROC\SOFTWARE
Sub-directories:   None

Files:             WP       .BAT
Path: \WORDPROC\DOCS
Sub-directories:   LETTERS
                   MANUSCRP

Files:             None

Path: \WORDPROC\DOCS\LETTERS
Sub-directories:   None

Files:             MILLY01  .TXT
                   MILLY02  .TXT
                   GEORGE   .TXT

Path: \WORDPROC\DOCS\MANUSCRP
Sub-directories:   None

Files:             NOVEL    .DOC

Path: \SPRDSHT
Sub-directories:   SOFTWARE
                   SHEETS

Files:             None

Path: \SPRDSHT\SOFTWARE
Sub-directories:   None

Files:             SS       .BAT

Path: \SPRDSHT\SHEETS
```

continued...

```
Sub-directories:   None

Files:             TAXES88 .SPS

Path: \DOS
Sub-directories:   None

Files:             BACKUP   .COM
                   CHKDSK   .COM
                   DISKCOPY.COM
                   EDLIN    .COM
                   LABEL    .COM
                   MODE     .COM
                   MORE     .COM
                   RESTORE  .COM
                   TREE     .COM
                   FIND     .EXE
                   SORT     .EXE
                   XCOPY    .EXE
                   ANSI     .SYS
```

This display is relatively short, although even it would span about four screen
pages. TREE displays of the typical multi-megabyte hard disk are much
longer.

You can use the TREE display itself to visually find a file, but there is a better
way. Suppose you wanted to know if GEORGE.TXT was on the diskette.
You could enter this command:

```
A>tree /f | find /N "GEORGE"
```

This command tells the TREE filter to pipe its output to the FIND filter,
which will drop all lines not containing the word, "GEORGE." You would
see this display:

```
[44]                        GEORGE  .TXT
```

This tells you that the file is on the disk on line 44 of the TREE display. You would take this step first in case the file is not there. Because it is there, build a file of the entire tree with this command:

```
A>tree /f >tree.all
```

Use your text editor (EDLIN in Chapter 8 if you prefer) to look at the TREE.ALL file you just created. It will look just like the full TREE display shown previously. Use the text editor to move to line 44. Then look above that line for the first Path entry, which, in this example, looks like this:

```
Path: \WORDPROC\DOCS\LETTERS
Sub-directories:  None

Files:              MILLY01 .TXT
                    MILLY02 .TXT
                    GEORGE  .TXT
```

You know from this search that GEORGE.TXT is in the \WORDPROC\DOCS\LETTERS subdirectory, and you have found the file you are looking for.

A Directory of Today's Updates

You can use the FIND filter to control the DIR command. Suppose you have a subdirectory with a large number of files, and you are interested in those files with a certain date. Enter this command:

```
A>dir | find " 4-27-89"
```

This command will display a directory of only those files with a date of April 27, 1989.

Sorting the Directory by Date

The SORT filter sorts a file on a selected field. The field begins in each line with the column you specify in the /+ option (or column 1 if you specify no /+ option). This limited sorting procedure does not allow you to sort on multiple fields. For example, if you want to sort a directory on the file date, you cannot because the month and day come before the year. The Januaries would sort together ahead of the Februaries, regardless of the years. If you know the range of years in your directories, you can use filters in a batch file to get a sorted directory. Assume for this exercise that your directories go no farther back than 1987. Using the COPY CON command, build this batch file named SD.BAT:

```
dir | find "-87" >87.dir
dir | find "-88" >88.dir
dir | find "-89" >89.dir
sort <87.dir /+24 >all.dir
sort <88.dir /+24 >>all.dir
sort <89.dir /+24 >>all.dir
more <all.dir
del *.dir
```

Press F6 and then the Enter key.

To view a sorted directory of files dated within the last three years, enter the SD command. Here is how it works.

The three DIR commands build three files. The first DIR command builds 87.DIR, which contains a directory of all files with dates from 1987. The second DIR command builds 88.DIR, and the third DIR command builds 89.DIR.

The three SORT commands sort the three files by date, which starts in the 24th position of a directory entry. The second and third sorted directories are appended to the file named ALL.DIR, which is created by the first SORT command. The ALL.DIR file is displayed on the screen through the MORE filter, and then all the .DIR files created by this procedure are deleted.

Timing an Operation

Some PC processes take a while. You might be posting your month's accounting journals or doing a cyclic data base backup operation. Perhaps you'd like a record of how long one of these extended, unattended operations takes so that you'll know how much time to set aside the next time. Maybe you do not want to hang around with a stop watch waiting for the run to complete. You'd rather go to lunch.

One way to time an operation is to allow DOS to do it for you. As an example, suppose your extended program is called DOIT. You can build the following batch file to record the start time in a file, execute your DOIT program, and record the stop time. When you get back from lunch, you can use the TYPE command to see the two times.

Because the TIME command expects a keyboard entry and will wait for one, you must use input redirection to give it one. Build a file named ENTER with this command.

```
A>copy con enter
```

(Remember to press the Enter key at the end of the above command line.) Press the Enter key again, the F6 key, and the Enter key one more time. You have just built a file with an Enter keystroke in it. This file can be read by the DATE and TIME commands.

Now build the batch file named TIMEIT.BAT with this command:

```
A>copy con timeit.bat
```

Enter these lines (remember to press Enter at the end of each line):

```
echo ---- START TIME ----
date <enter >elapsed
time <enter >>elapsed
call doit
echo ---- STOP TIME ----
date <enter >>elapsed
time <enter >>elapsed
type elapsed
```

Press F6 and then Enter. Run your timed operation by entering the TIMEIT command. When you return and when the job is done, the start and stop times are on the screen in this format:

```
A>type elapsed
---- START TIME ----
Current date is Sat  4-29-1989
Enter new date (mm-dd-yy):
Current time is 12:26:01.97
Enter new time:
---- STOP TIME ----
Current date is Sat  4-29-1989
Enter new date (mm-dd-yy):
Current time is 12:30:03.72
Enter new time:
```

With some simple arithmetic, you can compute your elapsed time for the job.

Note that the TIMEIT.BAT command does not work if the DOIT command is a batch file unless you are using DOS version 3.3 or newer. In earlier versions of DOS, a batch file can call another batch file only as the last thing it does. Beginning with DOS 3.3, if a batch file calls another batch file, the calling batch file is resumed when the called batch file is done. If the DOIT command is a .COM or .EXE file, the DOIT command would not have the CALL prefix.

SUMMARY

This chapter began Section II, the Power User's introduction. It explained the DOS pipes, filters, and input/output redirection. Chapter 7 is a brief description of the DOS commands used by a Power User. There are no exercises in Chapter 7, but there are examples and illustrations.

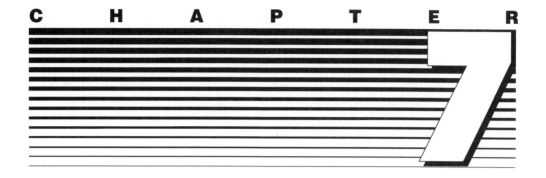

ADVANCED TOPICS AND COMMANDS

This chapter discusses some of the advanced uses of DOS. These are the toys and tools of the Power User, and you should learn about them so you'll be able to recognize a need for them in the future. You will not engage in exhaustive exercises in this chapter. Its purpose is to expose you to these subjects rather than to intensively school you in them. Later, when you need some of these features, the subject matter in this chapter will help you to identify them. By then you will be qualified to use the more advanced books on DOS.

In this chapter, you will spend some time on the subject of saving and restoring your work. Of all the advanced subjects, this one is the most useful for the widest range of users.

What you will learn in this chapter:

- Advanced FORMAT options
- System configuration
- Saving and restoring
- Moving DOS
- Printing
- Disk management
- Environment variables

Not all the advanced commands are covered here. Many of them are too advanced for the beginning DOS user. A comprehensive treatment of these commands would be lost on a beginner, and a brief pass-by would not shed any light on their real purpose.

FORMAT REVISITED

You learned the basics of the FORMAT command in Chapter 4 when you first built the TYD Learning Diskette. You used the /S option to format a diskette and add the DOS system files to it. A diskette formatted in this manner can be used to boot DOS on any PC-compatible computer that has a compatible diskette drive.

The FORMAT command completely erases all data on a diskette. When you use it, make sure that there are no files on the diskette that you want to keep.

You can issue the FORMAT command to reformat your hard disk, but you seldom, if ever, want to do so. When you become a full-fledged Power User and system installer, you will know when and how to do this.

The FORMAT command has options other than the /S option. If you issue the command with no options, it will attempt to format the diskette in its default configuration with no copy of DOS added. A diskette formatted this way cannot be used to boot DOS. Furthermore, you cannot add DOS to the diskette without rerunning the FORMAT command against the diskette.

You can tell FORMAT that you are formatting a 5 1/4" 360KB diskette in a 1.2MB drive or a 3 1/2" 720KB diskette in a 1.44MB drive. You cannot go in the other direction for either disk size, however (i.e., you cannot tell FORMAT that you are formatting a 1.2MB diskette in a 360KB drive or a 1.44MB diskette in a 720KB drive).

FORMAT will build single-sided 5 1/4" diskettes, but there is little use for this format. Following are the FORMAT command-line options:

Command Line Option	Meaning
/4 or /F:360	Format 360KB diskette in 1.2MB drive
/F:720	Format 720KB diskette in 1.44MB drive
/V:label	Add "label" as diskette's volume label
/B	Format with room for DOS
/S	Format and copy DOS to diskette
/1	Format 160KB diskette (single-sided)
/8	Format 8 sectors per track

SYSTEM CONFIGURATION

When you load DOS, it uses two files to tell it how to set itself up. These two files must be in the root directory of the boot disk. They are text files that you build, and their names are CONFIG.SYS and AUTOEXEC.BAT.

CONFIG.SYS

All DOS systems should have a CONFIG.SYS file even though you haven't built one for the TYD Learning Diskette. When DOS loads, it uses the entries in this file to modify its configuration, adding device drivers, setting operating parameters, and establishing the sizes of internal tables. The entries in CONFIG.SYS can affect the size of DOS and can, therefore, affect the amount of memory available for applications programs to run.

Minimum Requirements for CONFIG.SYS

You build CONFIG.SYS with a text editor program or by using the COPY CON CONFIG.SYS technique. At a minimum, CONFIG.SYS should have these lines of text:

```
files=20
buffers=20
```

The reason you need these lines is that most applications programs require them. They specify the size of some internal DOS tables that influence DOS's performance in support of applications programs. Some applications programs require larger numbers in the statements. If this is true, the installation procedures for the applications programs will either say so or will automatically update the file to the values needed.

ANSI.SYS

DOS includes a device driver program called ANSI.SYS. You will find it along with the other DOS utility programs. Its purpose is to enhance screen displays and keyboard input and is of use to you if some of your applications programs require it. Many systems include ANSI.SYS just in case an applications program needs it. To include it in your system, add this line to CONFIG.SYS:

```
device=ansi.sys
```

If the file named ANSI.SYS is in a subdirectory other than the root directory of the boot disk, you must include the path in the CONFIG.SYS entry. For example, if your system has all the DOS utility programs in the \DOS subdirectory, the entry in CONFIG.SYS would look like this:

```
device=\dos\ansi.sys
```

When ANSI.SYS is installed, the screen displays of your PC react differently to certain sequences of characters written to the screen by programs. You can use this feature to modify the DOS prompt by putting these sequences into the PROMPT command. The most frequent use of this feature is to set the screen colors on color monitors.

With ANSI.SYS installed, you can use the PROMPT command in this format:

```
A>prompt $e32;40m$p$g
```

The $e is a special PROMPT command sequence that inserts the Escape character into the prompt. The 32 and the 40 are graphics codes that set screen colors. The 32 specifies green characters; 40 specifies a black background. There may be several of these codes separated by semicolons. The last code is not followed by a semicolon but is followed by the letter "m" to terminate the ANSI.SYS command sequence. The pg sequence tells the PROMPT command to display the current drive and subdirectory with each DOS prompt.

Following is a table of the values you can use to identify graphics codes (the example uses 32 and 40):

Color	Character	Background
Black	30	40
Red	31	41
Green	32	42
Yellow	33	43
Blue	34	44
Magenta	35	45
Cyan	36	46
White	37	47

Remember that there need not be exactly two of these values. You can add different combinations of these values to change the video effect.

Value	Effect
0	Reset to normal white characters on black background
1	High intensity
4	Underscore (Monochrome video only)
5	Blinking characters
7	Reverse video
8	Invisible characters

Other Device Driver Programs

Depending on its version, DOS may include other device driver programs that you might want to use. Your DOS manual will describe them in its discussion of CONFIG.SYS.

Other entries in CONFIG.SYS are dictated by the installation procedures of your applications programs and hardware additions. The most frequent requirement for CONFIG.SYS entries is the inclusion of device driver programs in your DOS configuration. If you use a mouse, a digitizing tablet, or other nonstandard hardware devices, they probably require a device driver program to be installed. The CONFIG.SYS entry for installing a device driver is the same as for installing ANSI.SYS.

AUTOEXEC.BAT

After DOS loads itself and before it turns the command line over to you, DOS executes a file called AUTOEXEC.BAT. DOS expects to find this file in the root directory of the boot disk. If no AUTOEXEC.BAT file is there, DOS automatically executes the DATE and TIME commands before giving you the command-line prompt.

The AUTOEXEC.BAT file is where you execute any commands you want automatically executed when the system starts up. The most common command found in AUTOEXEC.BAT is the PATH command that sets the DOS path to point to the subdirectories of all the software you want to use.

AUTOEXEC.BAT is where you put your PROMPT command, the MODE command, several custom SET commands, and where you load any memory-resident utility programs that are a part of your operating environment. MODE and SET are discussed later in this chapter. Chapter 10 discusses memory-resident utility programs.

Many users put a command in AUTOEXEC.BAT to start their applications program. If you use your PC exclusively for word processing, you might want to have it always load with the word processor program running. If you are working on a project that you expect will take a long time, you might want to have AUTOEXEC.BAT load the project's document file into the word processor. These comments are relevant to data bases, spreadsheets, and other applications as well.

Some users use a DOS menu shell program rather than the DOS command line, preferring to retreat to the command line only when necessary. Some menu shell programs even have a command line mode that makes the retreat simpler. DOS Version 4.0 has its own menu shell program, which is called DOSSHELL. There are also popular commercial shells such as the Norton Commander. If you use one of these programs, you might want to use AUTOEXEC.BAT to start it automatically when DOS is loaded.

You can put any command in AUTOEXEC.BAT that you can execute from the command line. AUTOEXEC.BAT can also use the special batch file commands discussed in Chapter 9.

SAVING AND RESTORING YOUR WORK

The most important task you perform with DOS is your work. Whether you are an accountant, a farmer, a writer, an administrator, a bookie, or a musicologist, your vested interest in the PC is in the data files you have created, nurtured, and grown.

If your most important task is your work, then your most important obligation is the protection of that work. Aside from the usual protection from vandals, plagiarists, competitors, and other low life forms, there is the requirement that you protect your work on the PC from the PC itself.

A PC is an electromechanical device subject to failure. The degree of failure and the degree to which you can recover vary. When a PC quits, it can take your work with it. Your only protection is a measure of prevention. If you make periodic copies of your work onto media that are separate from the PC, you have a form of recovery. Even if the house burns down, if you have copies of your work on diskettes (kept in another house), you can take those diskettes to another PC and resume work. The amount of real loss is a matter of how much work you have done since your last backup.

DOS provides a number of commands that help you make backups onto diskettes. These commands are discussed here. For most of these discussions it is assumed that you will normally keep your data files on the C hard drive and that you will make backup copies onto diskettes in the A drive.

COPY

You have already learned and used the COPY command in the exercises in earlier chapters. You know how to use COPY. Its most common use is to make backup copies of critical data files. Suppose your word processing documents for a project are together in a subdirectory on your hard disk. You can use COPY to make periodic backups of those files onto floppy diskettes that you can store elsewhere. If you have grouped them into files with a common file name extension—.DOC, for example—you can use this command to make backup copies:

```
C>copy *.doc a:
```

If your work involves different kinds of files (e.g., documents, figures, and tables), you could make a batch file named COPIES.BAT, for example, that had these commands in it:

```
C>copy *.doc a:
C>copy *.fig a:
C>copy *.tbl a:
```

(Note that the extensions used in these commands would need to reflect the extensions you used to name your documents, figures, and tables.) Most, if not all, of your backup operations can be done with COPY. You will need the other methods described next when your backup requirements become more complex.

XCOPY

XCOPY is an advanced form of the COPY command that became available in DOS version 3.2. (The version number where XCOPY was introduced can be different, depending on where you purchased DOS.)

Sometimes your data files are organized in a subdirectory structure. On the TYD Learning Diskette, you organized the \WORDPROC\DOCS sub-directory by dividing it into two lower subdirectories—LETTERS and MANUSCRP. XCOPY provides a way to use a single command to make copies of these sets of data files.

XCOPY will copy groups of files, including files in lower subdirectories, if you so specify. For this example, assume your hard disk has the same subdirectory structure as the TYD Learning Diskette. To make backups of all the word processing documents, you could use this command:

```
C>xcopy \wordproc\docs a:\ /s
```

This command will create two subdirectories, LETTERS and MANUSCRP, on the A drive and copy to them the files from the corresponding subdirectories under C:\WORDPROC\DOCS. If you want the target diskette to have the higher subdirectories (i.e., WORDPROC and DOCS), you must specify them on the command line as shown here:

```
C>xcopy \wordproc\docs a:\wordproc\docs /s
```

If you specify a different subdirectory in the target specification of the XCOPY command, that subdirectory will be created, and the files and subdirectories from the source will be copied into the new target subdirectory as shown here:

```
C>xcopy \wordproc\docs a:\newstuff /s
```

This command will create the NEWSTUFF subdirectory on the diskette in the A drive and will copy the files from C:\WORDPROC\DOCS into the A:\NEWSTUFF subdirectory.

XCOPY has several other command-line options:

Option	Meaning
/A	Only copy files with archive bit on; do not turn off.
/D:mm-dd-yy	Only copy files on or later than mm-dd-yy.
/E	Copy empty subdirectories to the target.
/M	Only copy files with archive bit on; then turn off.
/P	XCOPY prompts with (Y/N?) before each file copy.
/V	Verify sector copies.
/W	XCOPY waits for a source diskette to be inserted.

REPLACE

The REPLACE command (introduced with DOS version 3.30) is handy when you are dealing with a large number of files, only a few of which change at a single work session. It is also convenient when several people are working on the same project at different PCs and need to keep their collective copies of the work current. Finally, REPLACE is helpful when you are working on the same data files in two different locations, perhaps at home and at work, and you transport the changed files back and forth.

The REPLACE command matches the files in the source specification with files of the same name on the target specification and transfers the files according to how you tell it to. REPLACE has several command-line options, but the one you are most likely to use is the /U option, which replaces files on the target only if they are older than the matching files on the source. The effect of that option is that if you use the same diskette for backups, only files that have been changed since the last backup are copied. Consider the situation where you work at two different locations. While at work you modify some of your document files for a project. Before leaving for home, you make a backup with this command:

```
C>replace *.doc a: /u
```

The diskette now has all the latest files. You go home and transfer the files to the hard disk on your home computer with this command:

```
C>replace a:*.doc c: /u
```

This writes the changed files to your home computer. You can work at home and repeat the procedure to take the files to work the next day. Be advised that the two computers need to agree on the date and time for this procedure to work reliably.

Of course, you can get the same result with COPY *.*, but every file would always be copied, which wastes time.

The other command-line options for REPLACE are shown here:

Option	Meaning
/A	Copy only files that do not exist on the target disk.
/P	Prompt for each file before copying.
/R	Replace read-only files on the target disk.
/S	Search subdirectories on the target disk for matching file names.
/W	Wait for a source diskette to be inserted.

BACKUP and RESTORE

If you have a large number of files on a hard disk to copy to a diskette, the files might not fit. The COPY, XCOPY, and REPLACE commands will go as far as they can and then tell you they ran out of room. If you are using wild cards, you must then manually figure out how to get the remaining files onto the next diskette. The same COPY, XCOPY, or REPLACE command would not work; it would start over at the beginning of the list of files.

The BACKUP and RESTORE commands are intended to allow you to make backups of and restore large volumes of files onto multiple diskettes. These commands can be used to back up the entire contents of a hard disk, although that operation takes a long time and consumes a lot of diskettes. Many users prefer to use other methods to make selective backups.

To back up your entire hard disk onto a string of diskettes, you would enter this command:

```
C>backup c:\*.* a: /s
```

To restore those files to the hard disk, you would enter this command:

```
C>restore a: c:\*.* /s
```

Probably the best uses of BACKUP and RESTORE are for the nonroutine archiving of your entire hard disk and to make a temporary backup when your computer is going into the shop.

There are problems with BACKUP and RESTORE. Following is a list of them for you to consider when you are deciding if you want to use BACKUP and RESTORE.

1. The BACKUP and RESTORE commands do not work well across versions of DOS, so they are not particularly useful for moving the contents of one PC to another unless it is known that the DOS versions are compatible with respect to BACKUP and RESTORE.

2. Before running BACKUP, you must be sure you have enough formatted diskettes on hand. BACKUP does not tell you up front how many it will need, and it provides no way to interrupt and resume itself if you find yourself short on formatted diskettes. You might guess that you need nine diskettes, format ten to be on the safe side, and have BACKUP tell you, after it has written to the tenth, that it needs another. Your choices are to find another diskette or to terminate BACKUP, format an eleventh blank diskette, and restart BACKUP at the beginning.

3. BACKUP uses all the space on the diskettes. There is no easy way to tell it to preserve the other files on a diskette except with the append operation.

4. BACKUP and RESTORE treat the set of diskettes as one long logical file. To retrieve anything from this logical file with RESTORE or to append more backups to it with BACKUP, you must feed the program all the diskettes, starting with the first.

5. When you are using BACKUP to write to a large number of diskettes, you must keep track of the sequence and mark them as you go. Lose track of the sequence and the entire set of diskettes is useless to you. BACKUP provides no way for you to reconstruct the sequence once you have lost it.

DISKCOPY

The DISKCOPY command is used to make copies of diskettes. You will use this command to make working copies of the distribution diskettes whenever you get a new software package. You can also use it to make backup copies of any critical files that are kept on diskettes.

You do not need to format the target diskettes before you run DISKCOPY, and you do not even need two diskette drives to use the command.

To make a copy of a diskette in drive A to a diskette in drive B, enter this command (substitute a: for b: if you have a hard disk with only one floppy drive):

```
C>diskcopy a: b:
```

Follow the instructions on the screen, and it will be a snap.

ENVIRONMENT VARIABLES (SET)

Many applications programs use a DOS feature called the **environment variable**. Environment variables are text values that DOS stores internally and that programs can read. The programs use these variables to tell how you have installed the programs. DOS uses several of its own environment variables. The DOS PATH that you learned in Chapter 5 is actually an environment variable.

As an example of how an applications program would use the environment variable, consider this fact: An applications program cannot dictate the drive or subdirectory into which you will install it. There is no way for it to know that your PC has any particular drive or that another application does not use a subdirectory with the same name. Yet the applications programs often need to know where things are.

Applications programs also use environment variables for complex options that cannot be included on the command line. The installation procedures for applications programs will specify which applications need environment

variables and how to set them. You can experiment with these variables on
your own.

The SET command sets and displays environment variables. To see which
ones are set on your PC, enter this command:

```
C>set
```

You will see a display something like this:

```
COMSPEC=C:\COMMAND.COM
PATH=C:\WS;C:\DOS;\
```

The lines you see on the screen will depend on how your system has been
installed. This example shows two environment variables, one called COM-
SPEC and one called PATH. Both are used by DOS. To set one of your
own, enter this command:

```
C>set foobar=123
```

This command establishes an environment variable named FOOBAR that
has the value 123. Any program can read this value and modify its own
behavior accordingly. If you issued the SET command by itself now, you
would see this display:

```
COMSPEC=C:\COMMAND.COM
PATH=C:\WS;C:\DOS;\
FOOBAR=123
```

You can delete an environment variable by setting it to a null value as with this command:

```
C>set foobar=
```

PRINTING WITH YOUR PC

If your applications programs are installed correctly, they handle most of your printing jobs from within themselves, and you do not need to worry about how the printers are connected and what kind of printers you use. But DOS includes some printer commands that you can issue from the command line, and you might find use for them.

Normally, DOS is aware of one logical printer – the device it calls PRN. Your PC can have several printers connected to its printer ports, and the PRN device is associated with one of the several possible printing devices. To DOS there is only one printer.

Printing from the Command Line

There are a number of ways to print from the command line. If you want to print a text file, you can use the COPY command in this manner:

```
C>copy textfile.dat prn
```

You can tell DOS to print whatever it is displaying on the screen. Simultaniously press Ctrl-PrtSc (the Ctrl key and the PrtSc key) or Ctrl-P, and all subsequent command-line input and output will be written to the printer and to the screen.

You can print the file TEXTFILE.DAT in the example just given by entering this command. (Do not press the Enter key at the end of the command.)

```
C>type textfile.dat          (Do not press Enter yet.)
```

Before pressing Enter, press Ctrl-PrtSc. Then press Enter. The file will be displayed on the screen and sent to the printer. When the file is fully printed, press Ctrl-PrtSc or Ctrl-P again to turn off the printing of console input/output.

The technique just shown is handy if the file has tab characters in it. The COPY command does not expand the tabs into spaces. Many printers do not either. The TYPE command expands tab characters into spaces as if there were tab stops every eight positions.

You can use output redirection to cause filters to send their standard output to the printer. For example, the command just used can be entered as follows to get the tab expansion of the TYPE command but without displaying the file on the screen. By suppressing screen output this way, you speed up the printout.

```
C>type textfile.dat >prn
```

The DOS Print Spooler (PRINT)

When you used the COPY or TYPE commands to print from the examples given previously, you had to wait until the file was printed before you could use the PC for anything else.

DOS has a command called PRINT. With it you can send text files to the printer. While the files are being printed, you can do other work at the PC.

If you have a long document to print from your word processor, you can tell the word processor software to send the printout to a file rather than to the printer. (Many word processor programs have this feature.) Then, you can exit the word processor and use the PRINT command to print the file. As soon as it starts printing, you can return to the word processor or any other program. Printing goes on while you use the PC for other jobs.

Some word processor programs have their own background printing operations. You can continue to do word processing while they run, but you cannot exit the word processor to run other jobs until the printing is complete.

To print a file, enter this command:

```
C>print textfile.dat
```

You can build up a queue of files to be printed by issuing several successive PRINT commands. To see which files are in the print queue, enter the PRINT command with no parameters. To cancel a file (TEXTFILE.DAT in this example) from the print queue, enter this command:

```
C>print textfile.dat /c
```

The following command cancels all jobs in the print queue:

```
C>print /t
```

There are other PRINT command-line options related to buffer sizes and internal timing operations. The DOS user's manual attempts to explain them, but an understanding of them defies explanation unless you are a computer programmer. If the PRINT command either slows down your other jobs or prints the files too slowly, then changing these options might help. Here is a summary of the PRINT command options:

Option	Meaning
/B:*nnn*	Set the buffer size to *nnn* (512-16,000 characters)
/M:*n*	Set the number of ticks to print characters to *n* (1-255)
/U:*n*	Set the number of ticks to wait for the printer to *n* (1-255)
/S:*n*	Set the time slice to *n* (1-255)

The PRINT command loads a memory-resident program. Once loaded, this program remains in memory. You should not run this program for the first time from inside an applications program—that is, when you have temporarily exited to DOS while an applications program is still running (e.g., this is an option in WordPerfect). You should run it the first time from the DOS command line with nothing else going on. Once you have started up the print command program, you can make subsequent calls to it from anywhere (e.g., you can use it from within applications programs).

Printing the Screen

You can send an image of the screen to the printer at any time by pressing the Shift-PrtSc combination on the older keyboards or by pressing the PrtSc key by itself on the newer keyboards.

GRAPHICS

If your PC has a graphics video monitor, you can print graphs and charts on the printer by executing the GRAPHICS command once, then pressing Shift-PrtSc when you want the graphics screen printed. The GRAPHICS command loads a memory-resident program that senses whether the screen needs a graphics print or a text print and reacts accordingly. If you have a laser printer, be prepared to wait a while until all the graphics information has been sent to it. The PC will appear to be locked up, but be patient and things will settle out in a while.

DISK MANAGEMENT

DOS has some convenient commands to help you manage your disk system.

CHKDSK   The CHKDSK command tells you some interesting things about a disk and about DOS's memory usage. To run it, you execute the command with some optional command-line parameters. Enter this command to see the basic CHKDSK report:

```
C>chkdsk
```

You will see a display like this:

```
21309440 bytes total disk space
   38912 bytes in 2 hidden files
  102400 bytes in 43 directories
14780416 bytes in 1092 user files
   10240 bytes in bad sectors
 6377472 bytes available on disk

  655360 bytes total memory
  606464 bytes free
```

The numbers will vary depending on your computer's memory size and the size of your hard disk.

If your disk has what DOS calls "lost clusters," you will see this display ahead of the one shown above:

```
Errors found, F parameter not specified.
Corrections will not be written to disk.

4 lost clustors found in 4 chains.
Convert lost chains to files (Y/N)?
```

Answer with "N," and you will see this display:

```
8192 bytes disk space
  would be freed.
```

Now rerun the CHKDSK command this way:

```
C>chkdsk /f
```

You will see this display:

```
4 lost clusters found in 4 chains.
Convert lost chains to files (Y/N)?
```

Answer with "Y." The CHKDSK program will assign file names to the lost clusters. The names will be FILE0000.CHK, FILE 0001.CHK, etc. You can use your text editor to try to look at them if you like. Some might have recognizable text in them, perhaps even something you thought you had lost. To recover the disk space for further use by DOS, delete the files with this command:

```
C>del file*.chk
```

Lost clusters result when you reboot or power down while a program has an output file open. DOS has not had the opportunity to associate the disk space it has allocated with the updated file. As a result, the disk contains allocated space not assigned to any file. The CHKDSK program rounds these files up and gives them names.

LABEL

The LABEL command lets you give a disk a label. The disk label is displayed whenever you use the DIR command on the disk. Not much use has been made of disk labels. No software requires them, and they are seldom used.

DOS displays the disk label whenever you execute the DIR command. If you put unique labels on your diskettes, you can visually verify that you have the correct diskette inserted by using the DIR command or the VOL command described next.

VOL

The VOL command displays a disk's label.

SYS

The SYS command moves the current copy of DOS onto the disk specified in a command-line parameter as shown here:

```
C>sys a:
```

The target disk must have been formatted with the /S or /B FORMAT options. You might use this command to build a boot diskette. If you wanted to upgrade your hard disk to a new version of DOS, you could boot from the new DOS distribution diskette and run this command:

```
A>sys c:
```

Then you must copy COMMAND.COM from the diskette to the hard disk's root directory and the DOS utility programs from the diskette (there may be two or more diskettes involved) to the DOS subdirectory on the hard disk.

SUMMARY

This concludes the discussion of advanced DOS commands and features. The next chapter briefly addresses EDLIN, the text editor that is included with DOS.

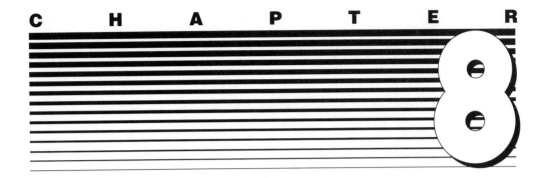

EDLIN

This chapter is about EDLIN, the small text editor program that is included as a part of DOS. If you already have an editor program that you like, skip this chapter altogether. If you do not, then proceed. You will need some kind of editor for the exercises in Chapter 9 when you build and test DOS batch files.

This chapter teaches you just enough about EDLIN to get you by. You will surely abandon EDLIN the first time you see a full-screen text editor (see Chapter 10 for some suggestions), but there are sound reasons to know EDLIN. For example, you might find yourself away from your own computer with none of your own software. A friend is asking you to help with a problem on his or her PC, and the problem involves some text editing. Perhaps you need to modify CONFIG.SYS and AUTOEXEC.BAT to install some software for your friend. All DOS installations have EDLIN. If you know how to use EDLIN, you can get the job done.

What you will learn in this chapter:

- Creating a file
- Simple corrections

SETTING UP THE EDLIN EXERCISES

You will use the TYD Learning Diskette for the exercises in this chapter. Begin by booting DOS. Insert the diskette in the A drive and press Ctrl-Alt-Del.

The AUTOEXEC.BAT file already has a path to \DOS set up, and you copied EDLIN.COM into the \DOS subdirectory, so the environment is ready. Make a subdirectory for your EDLIN practice exercises and change to that subdirectory with these commands:

```
A>md \text
A>cd \text
```

EDITING A FILE WITH EDLIN

Start EDLIN by typing its name and then typing the name of the file you want to edit. For this exercise you will create and modify a new file called TEST.TXT.

Building a New File

Enter this command:

```
A>edlin test.txt
```

You will see this display:

```
New file
*
```

The asterisk is the EDLIN prompt (similar to the drive prompt at the DOS command line). You will see it in two modes. In this mode, the asterisk is at the left margin of the screen. This mode is the EDLIN command mode. You enter EDLIN commands at this prompt.

Inserting New Text

You want to build a new text file, so you need to insert some text. The command for inserting text is the letter I. Press the I key now (upper- or lowercase works). You will see this display.

```
    *i
            1:*
```

The 1:* is the line number followed by the text mode prompt. EDLIN is waiting for some text to be entered. This is the second mode of EDLIN. Type a line of text as shown in the next display. You can use the Backspace key to make corrections while you type. To reject a line and start over, press the Esc key. Press the Enter key when you are done with a line.

```
    *i
            1:*Harry looked at his Rolex.  Time was running out.  the
            2:*
```

The 2:* is the prompt for line 2. Enter more lines of text until you have a paragraph as shown in the next display. Notice that the word "oficer" on line 3 is misspelled. This is an intentional error that you will correct soon.

```
1:*Harry looked at his Rolex.  Time was running out.  the
2:*fat man would be arriving at the rear of the bank any
3:*time now, and the bank oficer still didn't have the
4:*safe open.  Harry stretched his head around the counter
5:*and saw that Gilly had all the tellers and customers
6:*laid out on the floor, their faces flush against the
7:*tile, their hands behind their heads.  What was taking
8:*this guy so long with that vault?
9:*
```

Breaking Back to Command Mode

After you have entered the eighth line, hold down the Ctrl key and press the Break key (or Ctrl-C). You will see this display:

```
9:*^C

*
```

The Ctrl-Break key combination returns EDLIN to its command mode.

Editing an Error on a Line

You want to fix that misspelled word now, and to do that, you must move to line 3. You can jump to a line to edit by typing its number at the EDLIN command prompt. Type a 3 followed by the Enter key. You will see this display:

```
*3
        3:*time now, and the bank oficer still didn't have the
        3:*
```

The first line 3 is the way it appears now. The second line 3 is where you make corrections. You can completely type a new line, or you can use the DOS command line edit keys (see Chapter 4, the section titled "DOS Edit

Keys") to modify the line. Use the F1 key or the right arrow key to copy all the previous letters up to the missing "f." You will see this display:

```
*3
          3:*time now, and the bank oficer still didn't have the
          3:*time now, and the bank of
```

Press the Ins key to say you are inserting text, and press the F key. Then press F3 to copy the rest of the line from its previous value, and press Enter to say you are done editing the line. You will be back at the EDLIN command prompt as shown here:

```
*3
          3:*time now, and the bank oficer still didn't have the
          3:*time now, and the bank officer still didn't have the
*
```

EXITING FROM EDLIN

You exit from EDLIN one of two ways. You can use the Quit (Q) command to exit without saving any of the text changes. You will see this display:

```
    Abort edit (Y/N)?
```

You can use the Exit (E) command to save the file and exit. Enter the E command now to save the TEST.TXT file. The file will be written, and you will be returned to the DOS command-line prompt.

MODIFYING AN EXISTING FILE

Start EDLIN the same way you did before with this command:

```
A>edlin test.txt
```

You will see this display:

```
End of input file
*
```

Viewing the File

The EDLIN Page (P) command lets you view the file. Press P now, and you will see the following display:

```
*p
        1:*Harry looked at his Rolex.  Time was running out.  the
        2:*fat man would be arriving at the rear of the bank any
        3:*time now, and the bank officer still didn't have the
        4:*safe open.  Harry stretched his head around the counter
        5:*and saw that Gilly had all the tellers and customers
        6:*laid out on the floor, their faces flush against the
        7:*tile, their hands behind their heads.  What was taking
        8:*this guy so long with that vault?
*
```

You can use more P commands to view successive pages in a larger file. Each P command advances the current line to the last line displayed. To view the page containing the current line, use the List Lines (L) command with no parameters. Use a line number ahead of the P to start the page display with a particular line.

Deleting a Line

Use the D command to delete the current line. EDLIN does not always make it obvious what the current line is, so it is best to prefix the D with the line number of the line you want to delete.

To delete the sixth line, enter this command:

```
*6d
```

Enter this command to see the results of the delete:

```
*1p
```

The above command says to display a page starting at line 1. You will see the following display. Note that what was the sixth line is now gone.

```
1:*Harry looked at his Rolex.  Time was running out.  the
2:*fat man would be arriving at the rear of the bank any
3:*time now, and the bank officer still didn't have the
4:*safe open.  Harry stretched his head around the counter
5:*and saw that Gilly had all the tellers and customers
6:*tile, their hands behind their heads.  What was taking
7:*this guy so long with that vault?
*
```

Inserting Lines

To insert a line ahead of a specified line, put the line number in front of the I command. To put the line you just deleted back in, enter this command:

```
*6i
```

Type the deleted line back into the file:

```
6:*laid out on the floor, their faces flush against the
7:*
```

Press Ctrl-Break (or Ctrl-C) to return to command mode and exit EDLIN with either the E or Q command.

INSERTING CONTROL CHARACTERS

EDLIN provides a technique for putting control characters into a text file. Control characters are character values that are not usually displayed or that come from keystrokes that mean other things to EDLIN. The most notable example is the Escape character. If you press the Esc key while you are inserting characters into a line, EDLIN thinks you want to abort (or cancel) the line you are typing. Yet some text files need the Escape character. In Chapter 6, you learned that you could control the printer if you could redirect the ECHO command and send the printer a sequence that starts with the Escape character. Now you will use EDLIN to build the BOLD.BAT file mentioned there.

Enter this command:

```
A>edlin bold.bat
```

You will see this display:

```
New file
*
```

Press the I key to enter insert mode, and type the following without pressing the Enter key:

```
1:*echo
```

You want to have EDLIN insert the Escape character next. First, press Ctrl-V (hold down the Ctrl key and press the V key), and you will see this display:

```
1:*echo^V
```

Next press the left bracket, and you will see this display:

```
1:*echo^V[
```

Finish the line as shown here and press Enter:

```
1:*echo^V[E > prn
```

Now press Ctrl-Break (or Ctrl-C) to get to the EDLIN prompt, and press E to write the BOLD.BAT file. Now when you want to put the printer into bold printing mode, you can enter the new BOLD command you just built. Remember that the Escape-E sequence is for printers compatible with the IBM standard printer. Other printers will have other command sequences.

If you use the TYPE command to look at the BOLD.BAT file, you will not see the Escape character. The TYPE command does not show Escape characters in the text. But it is there nonetheless. You can look at it with EDLIN by editing the existing BOLD.BAT file. It will appear as shown here:

```
1:*echo^[E > prn
```

You do not see the V because it is not in the file. The Ctrl-V is a key sequence that tells DOS that the next character is a Control character. As it happens, the Esc key and the Ctrl-[key sequence deliver the same value to the computer.

SUMMARY

This small introduction to EDLIN gives you enough knowledge to create and modify simple text files. If you feel the need to know more, your DOS user's guide contains all the commands, although it uses the kind of command syntax charts that are normally read only by programmers.

Every DOS user should have a good text editor readily available for those infrequent but necessary text entry chores that do not warrant the use of a full-featured word processor. Unfortunately, EDLIN is not a good text editor. It will do the job, and many users find it adequate, but a full-screen editor is far superior. These editors are sometimes called note pads and can be found in memory-resident versions that pop up on top of your other work. Chapter 10 identifies some of these products.

The next chapter is about DOS batch files and how you can use them to do some interesting computing.

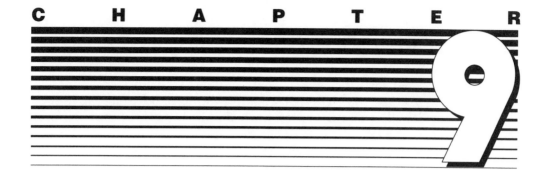

BATCH FILES

This chapter teaches you how to design and use DOS batch files. Writing batch files is an elementary form of computer programming, and it is remarkably easy and effective.

What you will learn in this chapter:

- What batch files are
- Command-line parameter substitution
- Suspending and terminating a batch file
- IF and GOTO statements
- Building a menu with a batch file

THE BASICS OF BATCH FILES

Batch files are text files that have the file name extension .BAT and that contain DOS commands. You have already built several batch files. WP.BAT and SS.BAT from Chapter 4 are simple batch files that you built to simulate some applications software on the TYD Learning Diskette. AUTOEXEC.BAT is the DOS startup batch file. You will be modifying that file in this chapter.

You build batch files with a text editor program. The EDLIN program described in Chapter 8 is such a program. When the file is complete, you execute it by typing its name as a command on the DOS command line. DOS then reads the file and executes each command in the batch file as if you had typed it on the command line individually.

Batch files have their own set of commands. By using these commands, you can build a batch file that uses command-line parameters and executes program-like loops and jumps, all of which will be explained in this chapter.

SETTING UP THE BATCH EXERCISES

The TYD Learning Diskette has most of what you need for these exercises, so you will use it. If you prefer to use a text editor program other than EDLIN, you should copy it to the diskette. You must put a CONFIG.SYS file into the root directory of the TYD Learning Diskette (use the COPY CON command or EDLIN). The CONFIG.SYS file should have the following entries:

```
files=20
buffers=20
device=\dos\ansi.sys
```

With the CONFIG.SYS file added, boot the TYD Learning Diskette. Make and change to a new subdirectory that you will name \BATCH by entering the following commands:

```
A>md \batch
A>cd \batch
```

For a test file, copy the NOVEL.DOC file into \BATCH from \WORDPROC\DOCS\MANUSCRP with this command:

```
A>copy \wordproc\docs\manuscrp\novel.doc
```

COMMAND-LINE PARAMETER SUBSTITUTION

You will begin with a small batch file that you will build on the TYD Learning Diskette.

A Single Command-Line Parameter

Use your text editor to build this batch file, named DOIT.BAT:

```
type %1
```

The batch file contains a DOS command to "type" something, or list a file's contents. The %1 is a special batch file token that is used for command-line parameter substitution. If you enter the command with a parameter, the batch processor substitutes your parameter for the %1 token in the batch file before it executes the command. So if you enter DOIT NOVEL.DOC, the batch processor translates that into TYPE NOVEL.DOC, which is a legitimate DOS command. Try that now with this command:

```
A>doit novel.doc
```

Multiple Command-Line Parameters

Now modify DOIT.BAT so that it contains these commands:

```
copy %1 %2
type %2
```

DOIT.BAT now has two substitution tokens, %1 and %2. As you might expect, %2 will have the second command-line parameter substituted for it. Enter this command:

```
A>doit novel.doc novel.sav
```

The batch processor will copy NOVEL.DOC into a file named NOVEL.SAV. Then it will TYPE the NOVEL.SAV file.

Every batch file knows its own name by the substitution parameter %0. If you use %0 in the batch file named DOIT.BAT, the DOIT portion of the name is substituted. You can use that parameter to display the command's name while the file is being executed. Change DOIT.BAT to contain these lines:

```
echo %0 is running
copy %1 %2
type %2
echo %0 is done
```

When you run the DOIT program, it will display these lines:

```
doit is running
       .

       .
doit is done
```

This is a convenience feature. Certainly you could put "doit" wherever you put %0, and the result would be the same. But if you ever changed the name of the batch file or copied it to another file name to modify and use it for a different but similar purpose, you would need to change all those "doits." If you use %0 to represent the batch file's name, the file automatically displays its own name, whatever that name may be.

PAUSING AN EXECUTION OF A BATCH FILE

Note: the following exercise assumes that you have a B drive on your PC. If you do not have a B drive, substitute C where B is used.

You can tell the batch processor to stop executing commands until you take some action. The PAUSE command is used for this purpose. Suppose you wanted your backup copy to be written to the B drive. Modify DOIT.BAT to contain these commands:

```
copy %1 b:
type b:%1
```

This batch file will copy the file you specify on the command line to the diskette in the B drive. But suppose the B drive has no diskette inserted. The COPY command would invoke a DOS error message. Or suppose you want to always verify that the correct diskette is in the B drive. If you fail to do that, you might copy the file to the wrong diskette.

The PAUSE command will stop execution of the commands and tell you to press any key when you are ready to continue. If you enter some text as parameters to the PAUSE command, that text will be displayed with the

PAUSE command. Insert the PAUSE command into DOIT.BAT as shown here:

```
pause Put Backup Diskette in B
copy %1 b:
type b:%1
```

Enter this command:

```
A>doit novel.doc
```

You will see this display:

```
A>pause Put Backup Diskette in B
Strike a key when ready .   .   .
```

Make sure that drive B has the correct diskette in it, and press any key when it does.

TERMINATING A BATCH COMMAND

The PAUSE command gives you the opportunity to terminate the batch file execution altogether. Press Ctrl-Break (or Ctrl-C) when it pauses, and you will see this display:

```
Strike a key when ready .   .   .   ^C

Terminate batch job (Y/N)?
```

If you press Y, the batch processor will terminate the batch job and return to the DOS command-line prompt.

TESTS AND JUMPS

A batch file statement can test a condition that you describe and jump to a different statement in the batch file based on the results of the test. If you have never seen a computer program, this concept might be new to you. Here's how it works.

Normally, a batch file executes each command statement in sequence, starting with the first one and ending with the last one. Many batch files are written this way, and, except for the command-line parameter substitution (described earlier), behave just as if you had entered the commands one at a time from the command line.

When you put a test and jump into a batch file, however, you allow the batch file to alter the sequence of commands that it executes.

Testing with the IF Command

You make tests in a batch file with the IF command. The IF command is not a DOS command that you would use from the command line. It is a batch command designed specifically for the batch processor. IF commands have this format:

```
IF <condition> <command>
```

When an IF command is executed, the condition represented by the <condition> parameter is tested. If the condition is true, the command represented by the <command> parameter is executed. If the condition is not true, the command represented by the <command> parameter is not executed. In most cases, the statement following the IF statement is executed next regardless of the condition. The exception is when the <command> parameter is a GOTO command, which is discussed later.

The < command > parameter is any valid DOS or batch command, except that pipes and standard input/output redirection cannot be used. You will often use the GOTO command as the < command > parameter.

The < condition > parameter can be one of the following three conditions:

- ERRORLEVEL < n >
- < string > = = < string >
- EXIST < filename >

The < condition > parameter can also be one of the above three parameters with the word NOT ahead of it, as shown here:

- NOT ERRORLEVEL < n >
- NOT < string > = = < string >
- NOT EXIST < filename >

The ERRORLEVEL Condition

This condition tests a value returned by many DOS and applications programs. To use it, you must know the possible values returned by the command executed just before the IF statement.

The DOS user's guide specifies the ERRORLEVEL codes returned by the DOS commands and utility programs.

The <string> == <string> Condition

This condition tests two string values. It is most often used to test the value of a command-line parameter against a constant string of characters. The command-line parameter is taken from the DOS command line where you ran the batch command. The string of characters is encoded in the batch file condition itself. The string can be one word only. Modify DOIT.BAT to contain only the following statements:

```
if %1 == novel.doc echo Oh no, not that turkey!
copy %1 b:
```

(The assumption is being made that you no longer need to be prompted for a diskette in drive B, so the PAUSE statement that prompted you for a diskette has been removed.) Enter this command:

```
A>doit novel.doc
```

You will see this display:

```
A>if novel.doc == novel.doc echo Oh no, not that turkey!
Oh no, not that turkey!

A>copy novel.doc b:
        1 File(s) copied
```

In this example, the command-line string entered ("novel.doc") and the condition string ("novel.doc") must be identical for the condition to be met. If there is a chance that the user will enter the file name in uppercase letters, you must test for both values, i.e., for both upper- and lowercase entries.

The EXIST and NOT EXIST Conditions

A batch file can test to see if a file exists. This feature is useful in preventing the execution of commands that require a particular file. You will find other uses for it as well when you begin to design your own batch files.

Modify DOIT.BAT so that it contains this line only:

```
if exist %1 copy %1 b:
```

Try the DOIT command with NOVEL.DOC and with other file names that do not exist.

Jumping to a Label with the GOTO Command

You can insert a statement in a batch file that is called a "label." A batch file can have several labels, and labels themselves are not executed. The purpose of a label is to give the GOTO statement a place to "jump," or go to. A **label** is a single word in a batch file with a colon as the first character. Following are examples of batch file labels:

```
:top
:wp
:exit
```

The GOTO statement has this format:

```
goto <label>
```

The < label > parameter in a GOTO statement must correspond with a label in the batch file. The label in the GOTO statement does not include the colon prefix that other labels have.

When the batch processor encounters a GOTO statement, it resumes execution with the statement that follows the label that matches the GOTO parameter. With this feature, you can cause the batch processor to modify its command sequence. When combined with the IF statement, the GOTO statement gives powerful decision-making capabilities to your batch file.

Rebuild DOIT.BAT to contain these statements:

```
if not exist %1 goto exit
copy %1 b:
:exit
```

Run the DOIT command with NOVEL.DOC and with some invalid file names to observe the effect of the IF test.

Complex Tests in a Batch File

You can have multiple IFs, GOTOs, and labels in a batch file. Rebuild DOIT.BAT to contain these statements:

```
echo off
:start
    echo %0 is starting
    if not exist %1 goto nofile
        if %1 == novel.doc goto nocando
            echo copying %1
            copy %1 b:
            goto exit
:nofile
    echo There is no such file as %1
    goto exit
:nocando
    echo I refuse to copy that turkey
:exit
    echo %0 is done
```

Following is an explanation of some style changes in this file.

First, the commands are indented. This technique makes it easier to tell where the labels are and which statements are subordinate to IF tests. The START label is included just to preserve the integrity of the indenting style. No GOTO statement references START. The art of indenting is a personal one and subject to your preferences and your eye. You will find a style you like.

Second, the file begins with an ECHO OFF statement. This tells the batch processor not to display every statement before it executes it, a technique that cleans up the screen display considerably.

The following commands and displays show three executions of DOIT.BAT, one with a file name that does not exist, one with the file named NOVEL.DOC, and one with the name of the DOIT.BAT file itself.

Enter the following command to try the DOIT batch file with a file name parameter that does not exist:

```
A>doit nofile.bad
```

You will see this display:

```
A>echo off
doit is starting
There is no such file as nofile.bad
doit is done
```

Enter this command to try the DOIT batch file with the file name that it rejects:

```
A>doit novel.doc
```

You will see this display:

```
A>echo off
doit is starting
I refuse to copy that turkey
doit is done
```

Enter this command to try the DOIT batch file with a file name that it will accept:

```
A>doit doit.bat
```

You will see this display:

```
A>echo off
doit is starting
copying doit.bat
        1 File(s) copied
doit is done
```

REMARKS

You can insert **remarks** into a batch file to explain its meaning. The REM command at the beginning of a line turns any line into a remark. Remarks are bypassed by the batch processor. If ECHO is on, the remarks are displayed as they are passed. Here is DOIT.BAT with some remarks and some blank lines inserted to make it more readable.

```
echo off
rem    ------ Start Processing --------
:start
rem ------- display the batch file name ------
   echo %0 is starting

   rem ------ test for the file's existence -------
   if not exist %1 goto nofile
```

continued...

```
        rem ---- do not accept NOVEL.DOC ----------
        if %1 == novel.doc goto nocando

            rem -------- copy the file to the B: drive -----

            echo copying %1
            copy %1 b:
            goto exit

    rem ------ No such file on the disk --------
    :nofile
        echo There is no such file as %1
        goto exit

    rem ------- refuse to copy NOVEL.DOC -----------
    :nocando
        echo I refuse to copy that turkey
    rem ----- all done ---------
    :exit
        echo %0 is done
```

NESTED AND CHAINED BATCH COMMANDS

Earlier versions of DOS did not provide for nested batch commands. A batch file could not call another batch file except as its last operation. However, beginning with DOS version 3.30, batch commands can be **nested** because batch processing includes the CALL command, which allows one batch file to call another and then continue after the second batch file completes.

If a batch file executes another batch command (which calls another batch file) without using the CALL command to do it, the execution **chains** to the other batch file, and the first batch file is not continued when the second one completes.

You will use the CALL command in the batch file menu shell exercise that follows.

ENVIRONMENT VARIABLES IN BATCH FILES

You can reference the value of an environment variable (explained in Chapter 7) in a batch file by referencing its name surrounded by percent signs. For example, build this batch file and name it HUNTPECK.BAT:

```
type %file%
```

Now enter the following commands. The first one sets an environment variable named FILE to the value "a:\autoexec.bat." The second command executes the HUNTPECK batch command:

```
A>set file=a:\autoexec.bat
A>huntpeck
```

The HUNTPECK batch file will substitute the value that is set in the FILE environment variable for the %file% substitution token. You would see this display:

```
A>type a:\autoexec.bat
echo off
cls
echo Teach Yourself DOS Learning Diskette
ver
path=a:\wordproc\software;a:\sprdsht\software;a:\dos
```

A handy use for the environment variable substitution feature is for extension of the DOS PATH. Often you want to add a subdirectory to the path without removing any of the rest of the path. Yet you do not want to type in the entire path every time. Build this batch file called XPATH.BAT:

```
path=%path%;%1
```

Use the PATH command to see the current path. You will see this display:

```
PATH=A:\WORDPROC\SOFTWARE;A:\SPRDSHT\SOFTWARE;A:\DOS
```

Enter this command to add a path to the \BATCH subdirectory you built earlier in the chapter:

```
A>xpath a:\batch
```

You will see this display:

```
A>path=A:\WORDPROC\SOFTWARE;A:\SPRDSHT\SOFTWARE;A:\DOS;a:\batch
```

The DOS PATH has been extended to include the \BATCH subdirectory.

A BATCH FILE MENU SHELL

This exercise shows you how some imagination and an understanding of batch files can be put to work to do creative things. You will build a menu system similar to the menu shells that you have been cautioned to avoid in past chapters. Now you are going to build one to see more of the power of batch files.

The menu you build will be in the root directory of the TYD Learning Diskette. It will execute the simulated word processor and spreadsheet upon your selections. To accommodate this new menu system, you must modify WP.BAT in \WORDPROC\SOFTWARE and SS.BAT in \SPRDSHT\SOFTWARE. Replace the TYPE commands in both files with PAUSE commands with no parameters (use COPY CON or EDLIN).

You will build four batch files in the root directory. The first is MENU.BAT, and it looks like the following:

```
echo off
prompt $e[7;20HSelection:    $h$h
cls
echo                          Snappy Computer Menu System
echo                          ---------------------------
echo                          1 = Word Processing
echo                          2 = Spreadsheet
echo                          3 = DOS Prompt
```

MENU.BAT is tricky. All it does is change the prompt and display a menu. The prompt is made up of ANSI.SYS controls to position the cursor and display the "Selection:" prompt.

The first part of the prompt is the ANSI.SYS cursor-positioning command string. It begins with $e, which the PROMPT command converts to an Escape character. The left bracket follows the Escape, and this sequence is the ANSI.SYS lead-in string. Next comes the cursor row 7 followed by a semicolon and then the cursor column 20. The cursor-positioning string is terminated by the H.

The next part of the prompt is the word "Selection:" followed by three spaces and two $h backspace substitutions. The spaces are to clear any previous selections that are rejected.

The effect of this PROMPT command is that every DOS prompt will start at row 7, column 20 on your screen and will have the word "Selection:" as part of the prompt.

You can test the MENU.BAT file now. Execute the MENU command from the DOS command line, and you will see this display:

```
Snappy Computer Menu System
---------------------------
1 = Word Processing
2 = Spreadsheet
3 = DOS Prompt


Selection:
```

Even though it does not appear so, you are back at the DOS prompt. You have changed the configuration of the prompt from inside MENU.BAT. To get the A > prompt back, enter the PROMPT command with no parameters, like this:

```
Selection: PROMPT
```

When you run MENU.BAT for real, the menu is displayed as it just was, and you want to enter 1, 2, or 3 to make a selection. The Selection prompt is really the DOS prompt, so any valid DOS command is acceptable. To implement your three selections, you will build three files named 1.BAT, 2.BAT, and 3.BAT. Following is the file 1.BAT:

```
echo off
rem ------- 1.BAT: Execute word processing from a menu
cls
cd \wordproc\docs
call wp
cd \
menu
```

The 1.BAT file is executed when you select 1 from the menu. It changes to the \WORDPROC\DOCS subdirectory and uses the batch CALL command to call the WP.BAT command. In your actual PC system, the WP command might not be the correct command to call your word processor, in which case you would execute the word processor program, using whatever command it requires (e.g., you would enter WORD for Microsoft Word).

The contents of the 2.BAT file are as follows:

```
echo off
rem ------- 2.BAT: Execute Spreadsheet from a menu
cls
cd \sprdsht\sheets
call ss
cd \
menu
```

The 2.BAT file is executed when you select 2 from the menu. It changes to the \SPRDSHEET\SHEETS subdirectory and uses the batch CALL command to call the SS.BAT command. As with word processing, in your actual PC system, the SS command might not be the correct command, in which case you would execute the spreadsheet program using whatever command it requires (e.g., 123 for Lotus 1-2-3).

Following is the the file 3.BAT:

```
echo off
rem ------- 3.BAT: Return to the DOS prompt
cls
prompt
```

The 3.BAT command resets the DOS prompt with the PROMPT command. If you are using an adorned PROMPT command parameter such as PG, you would include that parameter in the PROMPT command in 3.BAT.

Now start over. Enter the MENU command. You will see the menu again.

```
         Snappy Computer Menu System
         ---------------------------
         1 = Word Processing
         2 = Spreadsheet
         3 = DOS Prompt

      Selection:
```

Try the first selection. Enter 1 and press the Enter key. The 1.BAT command will be executed and will call your WP.BAT file. You will see this display:

```
      WP: ---- The Simulated TYD Word Processor ----
      Strike a key when ready .   .   .
```

Press any key, and the menu will return when the 1.BAT file chains to the MENU.BAT command.

Now try the second selection. Enter 2 and press the Enter key. The 2.BAT command will be executed and will call your SS.BAT file. You will see this display.

```
      SS: ---- The Simulated TYD Spreadsheet ----
      Strike a key when ready .   .   .
```

Press any key, and the menu will return when the 2.BAT file chains to the MENU.BAT command.

Finally, try the third selection. Enter 3, and press the Enter key. The 3.BAT command will be executed, will clear the screen with the CLS command, and will execute the PROMPT command to restore the default DOS prompt.

SUMMARY

You have now completed your *Teach Yourself DOS* tutorial lessons. You are prepared to go out and practice your skills with confidence and ability. The rest of this book is about little bits of information that can make your work with DOS easier.

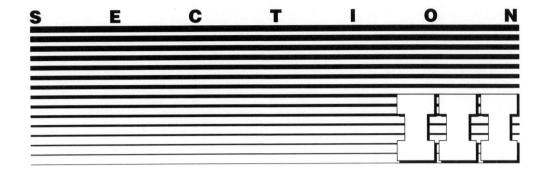

S E C T I O N

III

MAKING LIFE EASIER

This last section is to help you augment your DOS environment with some handy add-on programs (Chapter 10), and to help you figure out how to find some topics in this book (Chapter 11).

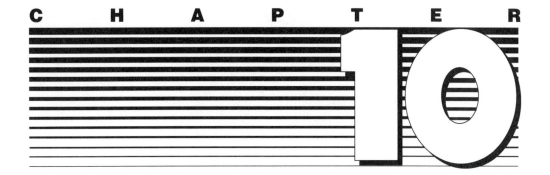

C H A P T E R

10

SOME USEFUL
UTILITY PROGRAMS

There is more to a well-running DOS installation than DOS and its utility programs. There is even more to it than your applications programs. Many software developers have added functionality to DOS with their utility programs. This chapter discusses some of the better-known and well-established of the utility program offerings for the PC. You will not learn how to use these programs in this book the way you are learning to use DOS. Each of them has its own user's manual. The purpose of this chapter is to reveal to you a small sample of the wealth of programs available to the DOS user.

These programs are all readily available from any computer software dealer. Software stores are springing up in shopping malls throughout the country, and most of them carry these packages and many other programs that are equivalent.

Do not misunderstand: This chapter, while endorsing these products, is not a paid advertisement. Furthermore, it is not being written with the sanction of or support of the companies who manufacture and sell the products mentioned. The author has used these programs for years and has confidence in them. There are others that are equally as good that do the same operations. Other users have their preferences. You should survey the field before you decide to buy anything.

SideKick

SideKick is the granddaddy of all utility programs. It is what is called a memory-resident pop-up program. You initially run it from your AUTOEXEC.BAT file, and SideKick is then forevermore available to you no matter what you are doing. Just press the Ctrl and Alt keys at the same time and SideKick pops up with a little menu that lets you select one of the following functions:

NotePad   The SideKick NotePad is a full-screen text editor program, the kind you were advised to look into when you were learning EDLIN in Chapter 8. The NotePad uses the Control key commands of the WordStar word processor, so if you are familiar with those commands, you can use the NotePad with no training. If you are not familiar with WordStar, the commands are not difficult to learn, and the NotePad will serve for all of your small text editing chores.

Calculator   The SideKick Calculator is an on-screen, four-function calculator with memory that you can pop up and use on top of any program. You can perform a calculation with the calculator and tell it to "paste" the answer into whatever program you are running.

Calendar   The SideKick Calendar is an on-screen display of the current month with the current day highlighted. You can move backward and forward through days, months, and years. You can select an appointment schedule for any day of any year and keep a record of your appointments for each day.

Dialer   The SideKick Dialer maintains your address book with telephone numbers. You can search for names and let the Dialer automatically dial the number if you have a modem.

Other Functions

There are other SideKick functions, such as the Help function that explains SideKick to you on the screen and the ASCII-table function that displays all the ASCII codes in a window. The Help function is augmented by a context-sensitive help system that displays a window of helpful information related to the current function whenever you press F1, the help key.

Vendor

Borland International
1800 Green Hills Road
P.O. Box 660001
Scotts Valley, CA 95066-0001
(408) 438-5300

SuperKey

SuperKey is a keyboard enhancer program, among other things. Its main purpose is to allow you to program keyboard macros. With a keyboard macro, you define a complex set of key values to a single keystroke. With this feature, you can assign routine, boilerplate key sequences to one key.

Keyboard Macros

In its simplest use, a keyboard macro lets you use the one key where many are usually needed. If you are writing a novel and the main character's name is Poindexter, you can assign the name to a special key combination, perhaps Alt-P. Then, whenever you need to type "Poindexter," you enter Alt-P, and SuperKey makes the substitution.

Macros can be more complex, allowing you to enter variable information from the keyboard and provide your own custom help windows.

Other Functions

SuperKey has other functions that you might find helpful. For example, it will blank your screen after a defined period of time elapses with no keystrokes. This action prevents an unattended PC from damaging the phosphor of the CRT.

SuperKey maintains a DOS command stack that you can use to review and re-execute previous DOS commands.

You can encrypt and decrypt files with SuperKey, and you can load completely different keyboard layout files.

Vendor

Borland International
1800 Green Hills Road
P.O. Box 660001
Scotts Valley, CA 95066-0001
(408) 438-5300

THE NORTON UTILITIES

There are a number of utility programs available that help you manage and diagnose problems with your disk system. The best known of these is the package called the Norton Utilities. This package comes with a host of programs that you use to rearrange your disk directories, find lost data, unerase files you erased by accident, completely reorganize your disk to speed up the access, and many other functions, summarized here.

Directory Sort   This program sorts your directories by name, time, date, or size.

Disk Test   This program tests a disk or file for physical errors, moves questionable clusters, and allows you to manually mark clusters.

File Attribute   This program displays, sets, or resets a file's attributes.

File Find   This program searches all directories of a disk to find files. It will locate hidden and system files that are not visible to the DOS DIR command.

File Info   This program lets you attach, edit, and view comments to a file name.

Format Recover   This program undoes an accidental formatting of a hard disk to make the data accessible again.

File Size   This program displays the size of disk files, the total size of groups of files, and total free disk space. It can also determine if the group of files will fit on a specified target disk.

List Directories   This program lists all directories in text or graphic format. It is used to print or create a file of a directory structure.

Line Print   This program prints text files by using a variety of formatting options.

Norton Change Directory	This program lets you change to a directory by specifying only part of the directory name. It will display a full-screen scrollable diagram of the directory tree. It also has Make, Change, and Remove Directory commands.
Norton Utility	This program lets you view and edit any disk area, unerase deleted files, recover lost data, and repair damaged disks.
Quick UnErase	This program will automatically recover erased files.
Screen Attributes	This program controls the display of screen colors and attributes if you have installed the ANSI.SYS driver.
Speed Disk	This program speeds up disk operations by eliminating file fragmentation. It alone is worth the price of the software package.
System Information	This program computes performance indexes of your PC and reports your hardware configuration.
Time Mark	This program gives the current time and date.
Text Search	This program searches for data in files or across the entire disk.
Unremove Directory	This program recovers a directory that has been removed and the erased files it contained.
Volume Label	This program lets you view, add, change, or remove a disk label.
Wipe Disk	This program overwrites an entire disk or the erased files of an entire disk so that deleted data cannot be recovered by someone else. It is a utility function to let you protect sensitive deleted data from being discovered by someone who has a program similar to the Norton Utilities.
Wipe File	This program protects sensitive data by overwriting selected files.

Vendor

Peter Norton Computing, Inc.
100 Wilshire Blvd.
9th Floor
Santa Monica, CA 90401-1104
(800) 365-1010

ProComm

ProComm began life as a **shareware** program, a program that you can download (through a modem) from an on-line service or an electronic bulletin board service, try out, and pay for if you decide to keep it. ProComm is a communications program. If you have a modem and want to access any of the thousands of phone-connect services, you need a communications package. The shareware version of ProComm is as good as any of the commercial packages.

With ProComm you build a directory of the on-line services that you want to access. ProComm will call the service you select, allow you to communicate with it by using your keyboard and screen, upload your files to the service, and download files that the service has to offer.

On-line services are the source of a great deal of free and shareware software. Such programs as PC-File, PC-Write, PC-Calc, and ProComm itself are available for you to try for the cost of a phone call.

ProComm is now marketed as a commercial package in its ProComm Plus version, with many additional features. But the shareware version is still widely available and will suit the needs of most users.

Vendor

PIL Software Systems
P.O. Box 1471
Columbia, MO 65205

ALMOST-FREE SOFTWARE FROM PC-SIG

PC-SIG is an organization that offers an extensive library of public domain and what is called "user-supported" software. Other terms for these offerings are "freeware" and "shareware."

For a small charge per disk, PC-SIG will sell you all kinds of different software. Some of it is in the public domain, which means that you can copy it, use it all you want, give it away, do anything with it at all except copyright it. The rest of it is shareware, which means that you can copy it, give copies to your friends, and try it out. Your obligation is one of conscience and honor. If you decide to use the software, you are supposed to pay a registration fee to its author, who is identified on the diskette. Shareware is a good concept that has worked well for many products, and you are the beneficiary of the concept. You can try out software for a small cost and buy it only if it works for you. If you decide to buy it, the cost is nominal. Most programs in the PC-SIG library have registration fees less than $50.

Among the categories of software offered by PC-SIG are the following:

- Word processors
- Text editors
- Computer language products
- Education applications
- Communications programs
- Memory-resident pop-up utilities
- Games
- Spreadsheets
- Utility programs
- Data Bases
- Financial programs

PC-SIG offers many such programs on over 700 disks. You can get it all on a CD-ROM disk if you have a CD-ROM reader.

Vendor

PC-SIG, INC.
1030 E. Duane Avenue, Suite D
Sunnyvale, CA 94038

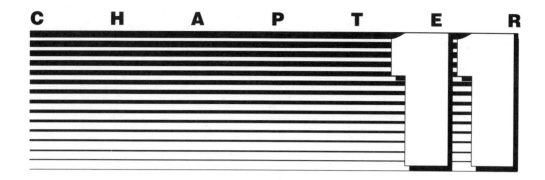

I WANT TO...
(AN INDEX TO YOUR NEEDS)

You will often find yourself saying, "How on this green earth do I do thus-and-so with this computer?" "Thus-and-so" can be a lot of things. No book can anticipate your every question or your every need. What a book can do for you, however, is teach you by example how to figure out a problem you're having. Your ability to apply the tools of DOS to the solution of a problem at hand is limited only by your level of experience and your imagination. Eventually, you will find yourself applying your knowledge of the DOS commands to the solution of complex problems. For now, browse through the items in this chapter. They are common and typical of the questions that most new users ask.

The next time you say to yourself, "I want to do thus-and-so," look to see if something resembling "thus-and-so" is in the list that follows. It is called the "I want to. . ." list.

To set up my system, I want to. . .

. . .get a new diskette to work

You have purchased a box of fresh, new diskettes, and they do not work. You get a "general device error" or some such message when you try to use one of them.

You need to format the diskette. Every new diskette must be formatted before it can be used. The FORMAT command is discussed in Chapters 3 and 4.

. . .add some new software

You need to read the installation instructions that came with the software. Most packages include an INSTALL command that customizes the software to your particular computer configuration. Others just have you use DOS to make subdirectories and copy the appropriate files from the software's distribution diskette to your working disk.

An important consideration is the DOS version you have. See Chapter 4, the VER command.

See also the discussions on subdirectories and the COPY command in Chapter 4.

. . .set and reset the calendar and clock

When you first buy your PC, the clock might be set to an incorrect date and time. Twice a year the time changes. Some PC's do not have constantly running clock hardware and must have their clocks set every time you turn on the computer.

See the "Calendar and Clock" section in Chapter 4.

. . .establish or change my system's startup configuration

You must modify the CONFIG.SYS and/or the AUTOEXEC.BAT files in the root directory of the boot disk. Chapter 7 has a section titled "System Configuration" that discusses these files.

. . .find what DOS version I have

There are many versions of DOS, and sometimes you need to know which one you have.

See Chapter 4, the section titled "The DOS Version."

. . .upgrade to a new DOS version

The SYS command is discussed in Chapter 7 under the title, "Disk Management."

. . .modify screen colors

You can change the default colors of the DOS screen with the PROMPT command if you have the ANSI.SYS device driver installed. This procedure is described in Chapter 7, under "System Configuration," and tells how to use ANSI.SYS in this manner.

. . .add a subdirectory or drive to the DOS PATH

See Chapter 9, the section titled "Environment Variables in Batch Files" for a description of a batch file named XPATH that you can use to append to the DOS path.

. . .design my own DOS prompt

Does the bland C> DOS prompt bore you? Does the Power User in the next cubicle have a sexy multi-color DOS prompt with the date, time, and current subdirectory in it. Do you want to keep up with that Power User?

See Chapter 4, the section titled "The Prompt Command," and Chapter 7, the section titled "ANSI.SYS."

. . .see what the subdirectory structure is on a disk

The DOS file tree can be a big, complex structure. Many users keep a printout of their hard disk tree on the wall. If you are poking around in someone else's PC, you will need to know how it is organized.

See Chapter 6, the section titled "Finding a File on the Disk" for a description of the DOS TREE command.

. . .combine a series of routine commands into one

Chapter 9 is about the DOS batch file processor. Batch files can contain predefined sets of DOS commands.

To manage my disk files, I want to. . .

. . .copy a file

Learn the COPY command. It is discussed in Chapter 4. Why do you want to copy a file? Where do you want to copy it? Do you really want to back up your work instead? See the next problem in this list if you're interested in backing up your files. Do you need to copy the whole diskette or just some or one of the files? Look two problems down to copy a diskette.

Also see XCOPY and REPLACE in Chapter 7.

. . .save and restore my important work

You bet you do. See Chapter 7, the part titled "Saving and Restoring Your Work." The entire subject of backups is addressed.

. . .copy a diskette

Chapter 7 describes the DISKCOPY command under "Saving and Restoring your Work."

. . .find my documents and files

Where did that word processor put them? See Chapter 6, the section titled "Finding a File on the Disk." Learn the Change Directory (CD) and DIR commands discussed in Chapter 4.

. . .recover some lost files

Did you use the DEL command when you shouldn't have? If you've not done anything else to the disk where the files were, you can recover them. You will need one of the utility programs that has an Unerase command. DOS itself has no such command. "The Norton Utilities" is a package of such programs. It is discussed in Chapter 10.

. . .get rid of some old files

See Chapter 4, the section titled "Deleting a File" for a discussion of the DEL command. Perhaps you want to archive the old stuff first. See Chapter 7, the section titled "Saving and Restoring Your Work."

. . .change the name of a file

See Chapter 4, the section titled "Renaming Files" for a description of the REN (rename) command.

. . .change the sequence of a file

You can reorder the sequence of a text file. There are different reasons related to the nature of the specific file why you might want to do this.

See Chapter 6, the section titled "The SORT Filter."

. . .create and change a text file

See Chapter 8, EDLIN. This is a description of the EDLIN line-oriented text editor. For very small files you can use the "COPY CON filename" technique introduced in Chapter 4, under "Using COPY to Build a File."

. . .name a disk file

Every disk file has a name. Except for files that come with DOS and with applications and utility programs, you must give names to your files. You must devise a meaningful naming convention so that you can tell later what each file contains by reading its name.

See Chapter 2, the section titled "File Names. "

. . .find out what is in a file

See Chapter 4, the section titled "Typing a File" for a description of the DOS TYPE command.

. . .make, change to, and remove subdirectories

The DOS file and directory tree is your creation. You build it by designing, creating, and modifying the subdirectories of the tree and by placing files into strategic locations within the tree.

See Chapter 4, the section titled "Subdirectories."

. . .send screen output to a file

Do you want to get a printout of the screen? See Chapter 7, the section titled "Printing with your PC."

. . .display a long text file on the screen one page at a time

If you TYPE a long text file, it scrolls off the screen faster than you can read it.

See Chapter 6, the section titled "The MORE Filter."

. . .find the files created or changed today

See Chapter 6, the section titled "A Directory of Today's Updates."

To manage my business and personal information, I want to. . .

. . .keep my appointment schedule in order

Look into SideKick, discussed in Chapter 10. SideKick is a memory-resident utility program that gives you this function at the press of a key, no matter what else you are doing with your PC.

. . .calculate some numbers in the middle of something else

Look into SideKick, discussed in Chapter 10. SideKick is a memory-resident utility program that gives you this function at the press of a key, no matter what else you are doing with your PC.

. . .automate my little black book

Look into SideKick, discussed in Chapter 10. SideKick is a memory-resident utility program that gives you this function at the press of a key, no matter what else you are doing with your PC.

. . .jot down notes whenever they occur to me

Look into SideKick, discussed in Chapter 10. SideKick is a memory-resident utility program that gives you this function at the press of a key, no matter what else you are doing with your PC.

. . .cut down on keystrokes

Look into SuperKey, discussed in Chapter 10. SuperKey is a memory-resident keyboard enhancer program that lets you define complex keyboard macros.

. . .find which text file has my boss's address in it

See Chapter 6, the section titled "The FIND Filter." You would use FIND to search your text files for your boss's name. If there are a lot of text files, you could do it from a batch file. See Chapter 9 for a discussion of batch files. Once you have found your boss's name, you could use EDLIN or your word processor to search the file for the address. See Chapter 8 for a discussion of EDLIN.

To run programs in unusual ways, I want to. . .

. . .find out how long it takes to run something

See Chapter 6, the section titled "Timing an Operation."

. . .print something while I edit something else

See Chapter 7, the section titled "The DOS Print Spooler."

. . .execute a command that affects more than one file at a time

You need to use DOS file name wild cards, special characters that provide a way to specify a group of files.

See Chapter 4, the section titled "File Names and Wild Cards."

. . .execute a program that is stored in a different subdirectory

See Chapter 4, the section titled "Command Path Prefixes" and all of Chapter 5, "The DOS Path."

To extend the reach of my PC, I want to. . .

. . .call a bulletin board system

Look into ProComm, discussed in Chapter 10.

To find my way around DOS and use it well, I want to. . .

. . .correct my keying errors on the DOS command line

See Chapter 4, the section titled "DOS Edit Keys."

. . .print what is on the screen

See Chapter 7, the section titled "Printing with Your PC."

. . .change the disk drive prompt

See Chapter 4, the section titled "Changing the Logged-on Drive."

. . .copy DOS onto a diskette

Use the SYS command, discussed in Chapter 7 under the section, "Disk Management."

. . .see how much memory my PC has available

See Chapter 7 for a discussion of CHKDSK under the section titled "Disk Management."

APPENDIX

DOS COMMAND SUMMARY

This appendix contains a list of the most commonly used DOS commands. Most of these commands appear in exercises in this book. In this appendix, page numbers for each command's exercise appear in parentheses after the command's description. If no page number appears next to a command, use the index (under "Commands") to find a general description of it. Your DOS user's guide describes all of these commands in full detail.

ASSIGN   Make all references to a disk drive apply to another drive (p.242).

Note: The ASSIGN command was developed to support programs that do not allow the user to specify the disk drives where certain files are located. Few programs are developed today that rigidly insist that files be on designated, unchangeable disk drives. You would need this command only if you were running an older program that was not as flexible as those being developed today.

ATTRIB   Set and clear file read-only and archive attribute flags (p.242).

BACKUP   Make a backup copy of a disk (p.174).

CD   Change the currently logged-on subdirectory (p.80).

CHKDSK   Display the capacity and file utilization of a disk (p.182).

CLS   Clear the screen (p.47).

COMP   Compare two files.

COPY   Copy a file or device to another file or device (p.101).

DATE   Display and change the current date (p.49).

DEL   Delete a file or group of files (p.70).

DIR   Display the files in a subdirectory (p.56).

DISKCOMP   Compare the contents of two floppy diskettes.

DISKCOPY   Copy a diskette's contents to another diskette (p.176).

EDLIN   The DOS line-oriented text editor program (p.187).

FIND   Find text in a file that matches a particular pattern (p.143).

FORMAT   Prepare a disk for use (p.53).

GRAPHICS   Allow Shift-PrtSc to print graphics images (p.181).

LABEL   Write a volume label on a disk (p.184).

MD   Make a subdirectory on a disk (p.73).

MODE   1. Set serial port parameters.
                2. Change default printer assignment.
                3. Set screen display mode.
                4. Set printer options.

MORE   Page standard output to the screen, pausing between pages (p.145).

PATH   Set and display the DOS command search path (p.118).

PRINT   Print text files while running other programs (p.179).

PROMPT   Modify the DOS prompt (p.92).

RECOVER   Recover a file from a damaged disk.

REN   Change a file's name (p.109).

REPLACE   Replace files from one disk to another disk (p.172).

RD   Remove a subdirectory from a disk (p.77).

RESTORE   Restore a BACKUP copy to a disk (p.174).

SET   Display, establish, or change DOS environment variables (p.176).

SORT   Sort the lines of a text file (p.138).

SUBST   Make all references to a drive apply to a subdirectory.

Note: The SUBST command was developed to support programs that do not allow the user to specify the DOS paths where certain files are located. Few programs are developed today that rigidly insist that files be in designated, unchangeable paths.

SYS   Copy DOS to a diskette (p.184).

TIME   Display or change the current time (p.49).

TREE   Display the subdirectory tree of a diskette (p.154).

TYPE   Display the contents of a text file (p.62).

VER   Display the DOS version (p.48).

VOL   Display a disk's volume label (p.184).

XCOPY   Copy files and subdirectories (p.171).

GLOSSARY

This is a glossary of words and phrases frequently heard among DOS users. You will read about some of these terms in this book. Others are common parts of the DOS user's vocabulary. This glossary briefly explains the terms so you will know what they mean when you hear them.

The next time someone tells you, "I made a backup of the shareware, hidden, read-only, memory-resident, utility modem applications program from the root directory of my extended memory RAM disk onto the same floppy where I keep my text editor," you can use this glossary to figure out what that person said.

ANSI.SYS   This is a special device driver program. It comes with DOS in the file named ANSI.SYS. To use it, you copy the file into the root directory of the boot disk. Then you insert this statement in the CONFIG.SYS file of the root directory on the same boot disk:

```
device=ansi.sys
```

When ANSI.SYS is installed, certain character sequences, when sent as displays to the screen, control video characteristics such as colors and cursor position.

Applications program   An applications program is one that you run to operate your computing application—the reason you have the computer. The applications program is different from the "utility" program. Typical applications programs are word processors, spreadsheets, and data base management systems.

ASCII   This is an acronym that means American Standard Code for Information Interchange. It is a code that was established by the American National Standards Institute (ANSI) in their ANSI Standard X3.4-1977 (Revised 1983) publication. It specifies the character codes used by many computer and communications systems, including the PC. The ASCII character set uses numbers from 0 to 127 to internally represent characters in memory. It includes values for the letters, numbers, and punctuation characters common to most text-based computers. It also includes nondisplayable characters to represent the carriage return, horizontal tab, line feed, form feed, backspace, and a set of communications characters.

Text files consist of ASCII characters. You can build and maintain text files with a text editor program.

The PC uses an extension of the character set (the values 128 to 255) for graphics screen characters to build window borders, playing card symbols, happy faces, and other special characters.

AUTOEXEC.BAT

To load and run DOS, you need several files in the root directory of the DOS boot disk. AUTOEXEC.BAT is a batch file found in the root directory of the boot disk. It contains DOS commands that DOS executes when it is first loaded. This file is optional, but most DOS installations include one.

Backup

This is a term that means to save your files on separate media—usually diskettes—for safe storage and possible recovery after a loss. DOS includes a BACKUP program to assist in this process. The term, however, refers to any technique used to make copies of your files. The copies are called "backups."

Batch files

Batch files contain ASCII DOS commands. You build batch files with a text editor program. A batch file has the file name extension .BAT. To execute the commands in a batch file, you enter the file's name (without the .BAT extension) on the DOS command line and press Enter.

BIOS

BIOS means Basic Input Output System. BIOS is a set of programs in the PC's Read Only Memory (ROM). The BIOS programs manage the PC's hardware and are executed from within other programs. Users do not usually need to concern themselves with BIOS.

Bit

A bit is the smallest unit of information that a computer stores. It can contain the values 0 and 1. Bits are combined to form characters. One character consists of eight bits. The 256 possible combinations of ones and zeros constitute the 128 codes of the ASCII character set and the 128 codes of the extended graphics character set.

Boot   When you load DOS, you "boot" it. DOS is booted when you turn power on or when you press the Ctrl-Alt-Del keys together. Users often call this latter method "rebooting."

Boot disk   This is the disk DOS is loaded from when you boot. If the A: floppy disk drive has a diskette inserted during a boot, the PC loads DOS from the diskette. Otherwise, the PC loads DOS from the C: hard disk drive.

Byte   A byte is an eight-bit unit of storage. Memory sizes, file sizes, and device capacities are expressed in bytes, Kilobytes, and Megabytes.

                    See also "character."

Character   A character is the value contained in one eight-bit byte. You think of these contents as characters when you consider their value. You think of them as bytes when you think of the unit of storage. A byte holds one character.

Chip   A chip is an integrated circuit, a miniature electronic device that serves a specified purpose. It is made of a silicon wafer that has thousands of semiconductor logic circuits. The wafer is housed in a plastic case with conductor pins that allow the chip to be inserted into sockets or soldered onto an integrated circuit board.

                    The microprocessor is a chip. The math coprocessor is a chip. Internal memory is a series of RAM and ROM chips.

Clock speed   See "megahertz."

Clone   A "clone" is any personal computer that is not made by IBM but that can run all the software that runs on an IBM PC. Some American manufacturers have become so prominent with their PC-compatible lines of computers that their brand names have their own identities. COM-PAQ is an example. The term "clone" has come to imply

PC-compatible computers made from parts manufactured in Asia.

Command line   The DOS command line is on the screen at the DOS prompt. It is where you type in DOS commands. It usually looks like this:

C>

COMMAND.COM

To load and run DOS, you need several files in the root directory of the boot disk. COMMAND.COM is the program that DOS uses to operate the command line and process your typed commands and batch files.

CONFIG.SYS   To load and run DOS, you need several files in the root directory of the DOS boot disk. CONFIG.SYS is a text file found in the root directory of the boot disk. It contains parameters that tell DOS how to configure itself when DOS is first loaded. This file is optional but most DOS installations include one.

Coprocessor   See "math coprocessor."

Copy protection   Many applications programs are "copy-protected," a phrase that means many things. The purpose for copy protection is to prevent or discourage the use of the program by software pirates, people who copy programs and use them without paying for them.

There are numerous copy protection schemes, and utility programs to defeat copy protection schemes have proliferated. Copy protection is viewed as an unacceptable inconvenience for the users who own legitimate copies of the programs because of the problems involved in making backup copies of the software disks.

Most major software publishers have dropped copy protection because of the criticism the practice receives in the press and because of user complaints. Many users steadfastly refuse to use programs that are copy-protected.

Ctrl-Alt-Del   To reboot DOS, press these three keys simultaneously. This key combination is also called the "three-finger salute."

Daisywheel printer   A daisywheel printer prints by striking the paper through an inked ribbon with a fully formed character embossed on a removable wheel. The wheel resembles a daisy. Daisywheel printers are capable of letter-quality printing, which means that you cannot tell the result from that produced by a typewriter. Daisywheel printers are not capable of graphics printing.

Data base   One of your application programs might be a data base management system. Your data base is the set of files that contain records of information relative to how you use the computer.

Desktop publishing   Desktop publishing programs combine the text from word processors, the pictures from graphics processors, and the document specifications of the desktop publishing program to produce a publication-quality document, usually on a laser printer.

Device driver program   Some software and hardware additions to the PC include a device driver program. These programs are in files with the file name extension .SYS, and are installed by this kind of statement in the CONFIG.SYS file:

```
device=mouse.sys
```

DOS includes two such programs that you can optionally install. One is ANSI.SYS, needed by some applications programs. The other is VDISK.SYS, which is used to install a RAM disk on your PC.

Device names   DOS uses device names as substitutes for file names in many commands. These names are CON, PRN, LPT1, LPT2, COM1, COM2, AUX, and NUL.

Directory   Files on a DOS disk are organized in a hierarchical structure of directories and subdirectories. A subdirectory is itself a file that contains a list of the subordinate filenames and their locations.

The directory at the top of the hierarchy is called the "root" directory. All directories below the root are called "subdirectories."

With typical computer ambiguity, the term "directory" also describes the file list displayed by the DOS DIR command.

Disk drive   A disk drive is a device that houses a magnetic disk platter. The platter records information. You can remove the platter from a floppy disk drive; the medium is removable. The platter in a fixed disk drive is not removable. Many fixed disk drives contain several stacked platters to increase capacity.

Disk Operating System   DOS is the Disk Operating System, so called because it is disk based. The primary storage medium is a disk. DOS itself is stored on and loaded from a disk device. DOS is also called PC-DOS if it came from IBM and MS-DOS if it came from Microsoft or a clone manufacturer. These DOS makes are the same. Any of them will run on any PC or PC-compatible computer.

Diskette   A diskette is a removable disk cartridge. It is made of a flexible, magnetic oxide-coated disk inside a paper or plastic envelope. The disk rotates on a spindle and its recording surface is exposed through an aperture in the envelope.

See also "disk drive" and "floppy disk."

DOS	See "Disk Operating System."
Dot matrix printer	A dot matrix printer prints by forming its characters in a matrix of dots. Each dot is printed by a tiny pin that strikes the paper through the inked ribbon. Dot matrix printers are usually capable of near-letter-quality printing, which means that you can readily discern the result from that produced by a typewriter. Dot matrix printers are often capable of printing graphics pictures.
Editor	See "text editor."
EDLIN	The EDLIN program is a line-oriented text editor program supplied with DOS. See also "text editor."
Environment variable	The DOS environment variables are text values that you assign with the DOS SET command and that are read by applications programs. An environment variable has a name and a value. Applications programs react to the value assigned to the variable with the chosen name in a manner defined for the program by its documentation. The installation procedures for applications programs will specify the requirements for environment variables.

DOS uses two environment variables. One is the PATH variable, which tells DOS what drives and subdirectories to search for programs to run. The other is the COMSPEC variable, which tells DOS where to find the COMMAND.COM program (or a substitute) during a reboot. |
| **Expanded memory** | Expanded memory is a device that adds large quantities of RAM to the PC. The PC under DOS can directly address only one megabyte of memory, so expanded memory is mapped, one small page at a time, into some part of that address space where no conventional memory (RAM or ROM) is located. Programs that can use expanded memory will usually execute more efficiently in a PC that has it than in one that does not. Few programs |

actually require expanded memory; some can sense its presence and use it to advantage if it exists.

Expanded memory consists of a hardware expansion circuit board and a device driver program called the Expanded Memory Manager.

Expanded memory and extended memory, described next, are often confused.

Extended memory
PCs that use the 80286 and 80386 microprocessor have the potential to address more than one megabyte of memory, and these machines can have such extended memory installed. DOS, however, does not operate the PC in the "protected mode" that extends its address range. (OS/2 , however, does.)

If your PC has extended memory, you can install the DOS VDISK.SYS device driver program to use the extended memory as a RAM disk. Aside from that use, there is little else you can do with extended memory while running DOS.

Filter
A filter is a program that reads its input from the standard input device and writes its output to the standard output device. You can redirect the input and output of filter programs to devices, files, and other programs.

Fixed disk
See "Hard disk."

Floppy disk
A floppy disk is a diskette in an envelope that you insert into a disk drive to be read and written. It is a removable medium and is the primary medium for software distribution and backups.

FORMAT
Before they can be used, diskettes must be prepared, or formatted. FORMAT is a DOS command that formats a diskette.

Graphics PCs can display information in one of two ways: as text or as graphics. Text displays consist of letters, numbers, punctuation, and the special character set that includes borders, happy faces, and the like. Graphics displays can be pictures, maps, charts, and other non-textual displays. Graphics displays often contain text as part of the pictures.

Hard disk A hard disk is an internal, non-removable disk device, usually with much more storage capacity than a floppy disk.

Hidden files DOS can record files that are hidden on a disk — they do not show up when you issue the DIR command. There are no DOS commands to hide files or reveal hidden files. Some utility programs can help you do this (the Norton Utilities, for example).

You cannot delete a hidden file from the DOS command line.

Applications programs hide files for reasons of their own, usually as a part of some copy-protection scheme.

DOS includes two hidden files in the root directory of the boot disk. These are named IBMDOS.COM and IBMBIOS.COM.

Hot key You activate most memory-resident utility programs by pressing a key sequence that is set aside for the program. This sequence is called a "hot key" and usually consists of the combination of the Alt, Shift, and/or Ctrl keys along with another key.

Laser printer A dot matrix printer prints by using the technology of copier machines. Laser printers are capable of letter-quality printing, which means that you cannot discern the result from that produced by a typewriter. Laser printers are the mainstay of desktop publishing, capable of printing with many different character fonts and with complex graphics renditions.

Math coprocessor The math coprocessor is a device that can speed up mathematical operations in a PC. To be effective, the coprocessor must be known to the applications programs. A program that uses a coprocessor can perform mathematical operations much faster than a program that does not use a coprocessor.

Math coprocessor chips are expensive and do not provide any advantage to programs that do not need or use them.

Megahertz The speed at which a PC can operate is measured in megahertz (millions of clock cycles per second). It is the equivalent of an automobile's horsepower or a stereo's power output rating.

The first PC ran at 4.77 megahertz. Subsequent releases of ATs and 386 machines have progressed through 6, 8, 10, 12, 16, 20, and now 25 megahertz.

The faster a machine runs, the faster it will process your data. If you calculate a lot of big spreadsheets, a fast PC will make a difference. If you use the PC primarily for word processing, save your money. An eight-megahertz machine is ideal. Anything more is overkill.

See also "wait states" and "nanosecond."

Memory-resident utilities A memory-resident utility program is a program that is resident in the PC's RAM but that does not run until you request it, usually by pressing a key sequence, called a "hot key," that is reserved for the utility. The advantage of the memory-resident program is that it is available at all times, even when another program is running. The disadvantage is that it occupies memory, even when you do not need it.

255

Modem   A modem is a device that allows you to connect your computer to another computer through the telephone lines. You will need a communications program to use the modem.

There are many on-line services available by modem. Some of them, such as CompuServe, are available by subscription—you pay a one-time connect fee and then only for the time you use the service. Others are operated by hobbyists and are available for the cost of the phone call.

Mouse   A mouse is a device that you roll around on the desk to move the computer's cursor around. Many graphics, computer-aided design, and desktop publishing systems use a mouse.

MS-DOS   See "Disk Operating System."

Nanosecond   A nanosecond is one billionth of a second. It is a measure that rates the speed of memory chips. Typical ratings are 200 nanoseconds and 150 nanoseconds. The higher the PC's speed in megahertz, the lower the nanosecond rating of the memory chips must be.

Path   The DOS path is the route through the subdirectory structure that DOS searches when you command it to execute a program. You specify that path with the DOS PATH command.

PC-DOS   See "Disk Operating System."

Pipe   The DOS pipe is the mechanism through which filter programs are connected. The first program writes its output to the pipe, and the second program reads its input from that same pipe. With the pipe, the output of one program automatically becomes the input to another.

Pop-up   See "Memory-resident utilities."
programs

Prompt   The DOS prompt is the sequence of characters that DOS displays to tell you that it is ready for a command. Unless told otherwise, DOS displays the prompt as the drive letter of the currently logged on disk drive and a greater-than sign (e.g., C >).

You can modify the DOS prompt with the PROMPT command.

PS/2   The PS/2 is the new generation of IBM PC. To the DOS user, the PS/2 is the functional equivalent of other PCs. There are architectural differences in the hardware, but these are mainly of concern to those who set up the machine and add internal expansion boards.

RAM   Random Access Memory (RAM) is the name of the memory chips used in the PC for volatile program and data storage. When you turn off the power, the contents of RAM are lost, so it is used for temporary matters, such as programs that are reloaded whenever they are needed.

RAM disk   A RAM disk is a simulated disk device made from RAM. By including the RAM disk device driver program, VDISK.SYS, in your CONFIG.SYS file, you can install a RAM disk. To the applications programs, it appears as though there is another disk device and, sometimes, a reduction in regular memory.

If the PC has extended memory, the RAM disk can use it, thus not requiring a block of regular memory to simulate the disk.

You would use a RAM disk for temporary work files, ones that do not need to be saved when power is turned off. The installation instructions for applications programs will

257

usually tell you if the program uses such files and if you gain any benefit by using a RAM disk.

Read-only file   DOS can mark a disk file as read-only. You can neither delete nor change such a file. The program that creates the file might mark it as such, or you can mark any file as read-only or read-write by using the DOS ATTRIB command.

Redirection   Programs that are written to be filters read their input from the standard input device and write their output to the standard output device. You can redirect these devices from the command line when you run the programs. You can redirect the devices to files or other devices or to other programs by way of the DOS pipe.

ROM   Read-Only Memory (ROM) is the name given to the non-volatile memory where the PC records the BIOS. When you turn off the power, the contents of ROM are preserved. A program cannot change the contents of ROM.

Root directory   DOS manages disk files in a hierarchical tree structure of directories and subdirectories. The topmost directory in the tree is called the "root" directory.

SETUP   AT-class machines record the details of their hardware configuration in a special RAM that is protected by a small battery. When you turn power off, the battery preserves the contents of the configuration RAM. While power is on, the PC is recharging the battery. To change the configuration, you run the SETUP program. This program might have a different name, depending on where the machine came from. In some machines, SETUP is a part of BIOS. On others, SETUP is included on a diskette that comes with the machine.

With SETUP you can reset the PC's calendar and clock, tell the PC that you have added (or removed) memory, and change the configuration of installed disk drives.

Shareware

Most software is expensive. You buy it and try it. With shareware, you get it for nothing or for a small copy charge. If you decide to keep and use it, you register it with its vendor by paying a nominal registration fee. The software and documentation are usually all contained on a diskette. You can print the documentation and use the software. Sometimes you get a printed manual when you register the software.

The advantage of shareware is that you can try something before you buy it, and the cost is usually low, reflecting the low overhead involved in its distribution.

The disadvantage is that you have to wade through a lot of junk to find a gem.

Shell

A shell is a program that attempts to do better what the DOS command processor does. It tries to ease the process of issuing DOS commands and navigating through the file system. There are many such shell programs. DOS 4.0 comes with its own shell. Users who understand the DOS command line do not need a shell. Many do not like shells.

Standard input device

Filter programs read their input from the standard input device. Unless you specify otherwise, the standard input device is the keyboard. You can use input redirection to redirect the standard input device to a file, a device, or a pipe from the standard output device of another filter program.

Standard output device

Filter programs write their output to the standard output device. Unless you specify otherwise, the standard output device is the screen. You can use output redirection to redirect the standard output device to a file, a device, or a pipe to the standard input device of another filter program.

Subdirectory A subdirectory is a DOS file directory that is subordinate to another DOS file directory.

See also "Directory," "Root directory" and "Tree."

Surge protector Occasionally, the voltage from commercial power companies surges. A surge protector is a device that you plug into the wall and plug your computer into. It protects your equipment from the damage that such surges can cause. A surge protector is a wise investment.

Text editor A text editor program is one that lets you create ASCII text files. The DOS EDLIN program is a line-oriented text editor program. Other editor programs are called full-screen text editors and are usually easier to use than line-oriented editors.

Tree The DOS tree is the hierarchical file directory structure. To view the tree, you use the DOS TREE command.

TSR programs See "Memory-resident utilities."

Utility program A utility program is one that you use to perform a utility job, usually related to the operation of the computer. Other utility programs are used for small secondary tasks that support your applications software, such as pop-up calculators and calendars.

Version of DOS DOS has been released in several versions ranging from 1.0 to 4.0 (as of this writing). To see the version of DOS you are running, use the VER command.

Virtual disk See "RAM disk."

Volume label   A hard disk or diskette can have a magnetic label. You can read and set the label of a disk medium with the VOL or LABEL command.

Wait states   You will often hear the expression "zero wait states" in the explanation of a PC's processor performance. This means that the RAM chips can respond to the PC's memory accesses at the speed of the PC. When this is not the case, the memory circuits halt the processor with one or more "wait states" so the processor waits for the memory to respond. You do not often hear this measure expressed because it is considered a disadvantage, and the writers of advertising copy do not like to accentuate the negative.

Wild cards   When you call out a file name on the command line, you can sometimes include asterisks and question marks as wild cards to form an ambiguous file name. The usual intent is to specify a group of similarly named files as opposed to only one.

Windows   The Windows extension to DOS is an attempt to provide a common graphical user interface to DOS and all applications programs. You will run Windows for one of two reasons: you like it, or an applications program that you want or need to run is written to run only with Windows.

Word processor   A word processor is a program that lets you develop textual document files. It usually has far more features than a text editor program, with complex formatting and printing modes, spelling checkers, and other functions of use to those who write documents and manuscripts.

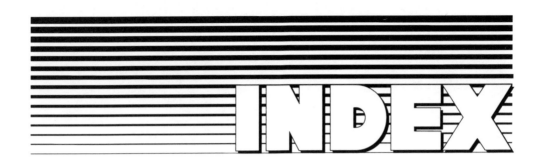

A

ANSI.SYS, 94, 166, 213, 233, 234, 246
Appending to a text file, 145
ASCII, 246
ASSIGN, 242
Asterisk (*) wild card, 67
ATTRIB, 242
AUTOEXEC.BAT, 58, 126, 165, 168, 198, 233, 247
AUX, 100

B

BACKUP, 174, 242, 247
BAT, 25, 247
Batch commands:
  CALL, 210
  GOTO, 206
  IF, 203
  Labels, 206
  PAUSE, 201
  REM, 209
Batch file commands, 28
Batch files, 197
BIOS, 19
Boot, 53
Bytes, 36, 248

C

CALL, 210
CD, 80, 235, 242
CHKDSK, 182, 242
CLS, 47, 242
Clusters, 182
COM, 25
Command line, 18
Command line substitution, batch files, 96, 199, 211
Command parameters, 26, 54
COMMAND.COM, 56, 185, 249

Commands, 26
Commands:
  ASSIGN, 242
  ATTRIB, 242
  BACKUP, 174, 242
  CALL, 210
  CD, 80, 235, 242
  CHKDSK, 182, 242
  CLS, 47, 242
  COMP, 242
  COPY, 58, 101, 170, 232, 234, 242
  DATE, 49, 55, 135, 159, 242
  DEL, 70, 108, 235, 242
  DIR, 27, 56, 134, 142, 235, 242
  DISKCOMP, 242
  DISKCOPY, 176, 235, 242
  DOSSHELL, 169
  ECHO, 61, 208
  EDLIN, 153, 187, 198, 236, 238, 242
  FIND, 143, 151, 156, 238, 242
  FORMAT, 30, 36, 53, 56, 164, 184, 232, 243
  GOTO, 206
  GRAPHICS, 181, 243
  IF, 203
  LABEL, 184, 243
  MD, 73, 243
  MODE, 243
  MORE, 145, 154, 237, 243
  PATH, 98, 118, 169, 211, 243, 256
  PAUSE, 201
  PRINT, 179, 243
  PROMPT, 9, 92, 166, 213, 233, 234, 243
  RD, 77, 243
  RECOVER, 243
  REM, 209
  REN, 109, 235
  RENAME, 243

Redirection, 136, 258
REM, 209
REN, 109, 235, 243
REPLACE, 172, 234, 243
RESTORE, 174, 243
Root directory, 30, 71, 258
Root directory, changing to, 91

S

SET, 176, 243
Setup strings, printers, 152
Shareware, 228, 259
Shift-PrtSc, 181
SideKick, 222, 237
SORT, 138, 158, 236, 243
Standard input device, 134, 136, 259
Standard output device, 134, 136, 259
Subdirectory, 71, 260
Subdirectory organization, 95
Subdirectory prefix, 96
Subdirectory, displaying current, 91
SUBST, 244
SuperKey, 223, 238
SYS, 25, 184, 233, 244

T

Text editors, 153, 260
TIME, 26, 49, 55, 135, 159, 244
TREE, 154, 234, 244
TYPE, 62, 134, 142, 236, 237, 244

U

User-supported software, 228

V

VER, 48, 232, 244, 260
Versions of DOS, 48

VOL, 184, 244, 261

W

Wild cards, 65, 261
WordPerfect, 18, 19, 181

X

XCOPY, 171, 234, 244